THE LUCKY ONES

On a terrible night in 1978, in a sorority house of a Florida university, 21-year-old Nita Neary stood motionless as Ted Bundy passed right by her . . . with a bloody club clutched in his hand.

On July 14, 1966, nursing student Corazon Amurao rolled under a bed and out of sight— and was forced to watch as Richard Speck led eight of her friends to their deaths.

Kansas 1974: After putting up a fierce struggle, Kevin Bright was shot and left for dead in his home . . . while BTK killer Dennis Rader murdered the young man's sister in another room.

Only a lucky punch prevented Tracy Edwards from becoming the seventeenth victim of serial killer/cannibal Jeffrey Dahmer.

THERE BUT FOR THE GRACE OF GOD

THERE BUT FOR THE GRACE OF GOD

Survivors of the 20th Century's Infamous Serial Killers

FRED ROSEN

HARPER

An Imprint of HarperCollins*Publishers*

HARPER

An Imprint of HarperCollins*Publishers*
10 East 53rd Street
New York, New York 10022-5299

First Harper paperback printing: July 2007

HarperCollins® and Harper® are trademarks of HarperCollins Publishers.

Printed in the United States of America

Visit Harper paperbacks on the World Wide Web at www.harpercollins.com

10 9 8 7 6 5 4 3 2 1

This one's for Dr. Richard Jewell at USC's film school,
who inspired me when I surely needed it.

ACKNOWLEDGMENTS

*E*rin Brown made this book happen. Without her intelligence, confidence, and considerable support, I would not have enjoyed meeting such fine people who have affected me so profoundly.

Jeremy Cesarec then did something I have never seen—he took over the project with the grace of a gentleman. That he happened to come from the same town as one of the survivors proved fortuitous and invaluable.

Will Hinton then shepherded everything through its final stages. His advocacy for the title made a difference.

Copyeditor Peter Weissman made it better.

Lori Perkins for the idea and support; Marty, Phyllis, Marian, Cal, Michael, and John for their caffeinated wisdom; and of course Sammy for the distractions.

CONTENTS

A WORD ABOUT SOURCES

This book is based upon an extensive amount of interviewing of the survivors of serial killers. Most of it took place in person, some through written and phone correspondence. Official, court, and police documents, including statements by victims and killers as well as trial transcripts, provided invaluable information. So did other background research materials, which are included in the Bibliography.

Direct conversations between the survivors and the author are recorded as they happened. Dialogue between survivors and the serial killers is based upon the survivors' recollections, which in each and every case matched all the known facts of the cases. On occasion the recollections of the same event between the survivor and the serial killer are different. In those cases, I have evaluated the competing claims and presented an account based on my journalistic judgment.

As the reader will soon discover, not every survivor wants to be found. In the few cases where the survivors did not want to be interviewed, I relied on the old-fashioned journalistic method of talking to people who knew them or of them, and going back to archival sources to build their profile.

In a few instances sources and interview locations were changed to protect anonymity. Likewise, the names of people on the periphery of the case. Everyone else is who they are.

PROLOGUE

*W*hen I was twelve I rode my red Schwinn bicycle out onto a one-way street. Too late, I looked to the right; a car bore down on me. As quick as the Flash, I peddled faster, hard as I could. I heard the car's squealing brakes, it was going to—

Suddenly, from out of nowhere, I sensed rather than saw it—a huge hand came down; there was a "bump." I fell to the asphalt. Next to me, the bike was a metallic mess, the front wheel spinning to nowhere. Still shaking from its forward motion, the car's front chrome bumper shone in the last light of dusk. Surprised to be alive, I stood up. Except for a slight scratch to my right ankle, I was unhurt.

Had I imagined it? Was it the hand of God that stopped that car before it could kill me? I have wondered ever since. Thirty years later the survivor of one of the twentieth century's most notorious serial killers described a similar experience, in which she too believed the hand of God enabled her to survive.

Surviving a car accident is one thing, surviving a serial killer entirely another. The very idea of surviving a serial killer was astonishing, considering the almost supernatural reputation they have developed. In large part that reputation rests with fictional portrayals, most notably Anthony Hopkins's Oscar-winning portrayal of Thomas Harris's urbane serial killer Hannibal "the Cannibal" Lecter in *Red Dragon, The Silence of the Lambs,* and *Hannibal.*

In the Millennium, Paddy Chayefsky's view of TV in *Network* has come true. Cable channels provide round-the-clock serial killer entertainment. So-called "profilers," self-styled experts on serial killers, comment on the serial killer case of the day. With their academic degrees flying, they assert that their discipline is the *absolute, positive, best* in understanding serial killers.

Someplace during the discussion with the over-anxious anchor who's feeding the profiler leading questions, humanity gets lost. Dehumanizing phrases like "dump sites," "kill totals," and "Fry him!" get tossed about. Amid all this sensationalistic "reporting," serial killers have gotten a popular reputation as efficient killing machines.

If they are so efficient, how come they always get *caught*? In many instances they give it away deliberately. Maybe they have grown tired of the game, or maybe they just want to die. Some are smarter than others, but they all have a feral nature that enables them to avoid detection. Serial killers have been born with some sort of gene that, at worst, makes them susceptible to developing a homicidal brand of sociopathy that enables them to observe others, emulate their behavior, and fit in.

What is consistent from case to case is that serial killers get a sexual kick out of killing. Forget anything they might want to do with the person before or after they kill them. It is the moment of death, which they think they control, that the serial killer lives for. What they don't understand—because they are so into their own perverse needs—is that sometimes their victim is determined to become their survivor.

Survivors of serial killers confront the most terrible, overwhelming evil imaginable, and live to tell the tale. Why are they so lucky? Or is it something else? Could God actually be at work in helping them survive? What about their lives afterward, their families? And what did they do with their second chance at life?

The only way to get the answer to those questions was to talk to the survivors themselves.

We are loved by an unending love,
We are embraced by arms that find us,
even when we are hidden from ourselves.

Interpretive Version: Ahavat Olam

THERE BUT FOR THE
GRACE OF GOD

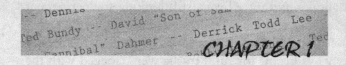
Survivor: Michele Chapman
Serial Killer: Derrick Todd Lee
aka "Baton Rouge Serial Killer"

"Maybe somebody out there may want one day to come to you. Chris not even gonna be in it because he's the detective. Your name gonna be in there because you the profiler."

—Derrick Todd Lee

New Orleans was easy to spot from the air. It was the big black hole where a city used to be, ringed by the lights of the surrounding communities that had survived Hurricane Katrina.

It was eight o'clock at night but it seemed more like two o'clock in the morning. When it was supposed to be bustling, the airport was comatose from inactivity. The place was totally dead, but that brought bargains, including a rented car that I could drop off in Texas for no additional fee. Outside, the roadways were empty, but farther north toward Baton Rouge, they became jammed with refugees. Many were driving back and forth over

Interstate 10, the main highway through the cane-brake and into Texas, still looking for permanent shelter and jobs. Trailers were everywhere.

Baton Rouge was a series of traffic jams. Road-ways meant for rural traffic were clogged with the hurricane refugees. The night was lit up by an endless string of white lights that outlined the giant oil derricks and oil processing plants in the west. A few miles farther up, the road split. I tooled my car off the interstate and into the canebrake. There were no street or highway lights. The sudden darkness was all-enveloping.

The canebrake is the countryside of Louisiana, Mississippi, and the Florida Panhandle that borders on the Gulf of Mexico. There was a time, from about 1929 until 2005, that no real storm struck the canebrake with the kind of force to literally destroy it. That changed with Katrina.

The hulking shapes in the darkness turned out to be shattered buildings and uprooted trees. The best thing to do would be to give Louisiana back to the French for the same $15 million Thomas Jefferson paid for it originally. After all, the Catholic parish system that delineates the state's infrastructure is a throwback to France's controls of the state. In Louisiana, parishes substitute for counties.

Suddenly, winged angels lit up the rutted four-lane highway with sharp white light. They seemed totally out of place, their spiritual promise and cheeriness in direct contradiction to the leering neon of the barbecue joints, sleazy video stores, and bars that stood behind them. The angels disappeared between towns, swallowed up in the darkness of the Louisiana canebrake.

The sign up ahead said ST. FRANCISVILLE PARISH—5 MILES. It was there Derrick Todd Lee was born in 1968. Fifteen years later as a teenager, Lee climbed a pole in the parish. When he got to the top, he had a great view of a second-floor apartment in the development. Inside, as he watched, beautiful young Patricia Savage began to undress. He looked at her unfolding body as something he just had to have, to hold, to contain, to control, to do with as he would.

Down to nothing, Savage looked up moments later to the incongruous site of a pudgy young black boy clinging to a nearby light pole looking straight at her. From the pole, Lee could see her picking up the phone. He tried to scamper down, to jump off the pole and get away, but his legs got caught on something. Police arrived moments later to begin what for Lee became the first in a string of lengthy juvenile arrests that made him a familiar character around the halls of the Zachary Police Department, which administered the law in the parish.

By 1989, when Lee turned twenty-one, he seemed to have turned a corner. Through charm and perhaps guile, he had become a well-liked member of his community. He wasn't well-educated, having barely survived high school. Derrick wasn't much into religion. He had become a concrete finisher whose talent and skills were in demand. As for his friends, they considered him a slick Casanova who was never without a woman. Lee flirted with anything in a skirt. It was just a matter of time.

In November 1992, at the age of twenty-four, Lee committed his first "adult" crime. Still favoring his childhood conveyance, bike riding was the way Lee got around. Biking through the Fenwood Hills neighborhood of Zachary, he found a house that looked empty. Parking in the front yard of Rob Benge's house, Lee barged into the house without knocking. Behind him, the kitchen door was left wide open.

Returning from a shopping trip, Benge was surprised when Lee, a handsome, massive African American who looks like the actor Michael Clarke Duncan from *The Green Mile,* came out of his bedroom with a friendly handshake.

"I'm looking for a party named Monroe," said Lee, turning on the oily charm and shaking the stunned man's hand.

But it was Lee who was surprised when Benge picked up the phone and called the police. Lee ran into a place he would come to know quite well: the Azalea Rest Cemetery. He tried hiding behind some gravestones, where his massive form was not easily concealed. It was no surprise when the police found him a short time later. Captured, he was taken meekly into custody.

Minutes later I spotted lights in the distance. Getting closer, the headlights picked out a weathered sign that said, ZACHARY—TOWN LIMIT. The angels flew in once again to the side of the road, lighting up the town that resolved itself out of the darkness.

A church steeple appeared in the town square. It was its huge size that caught the eye, more so than its dark silhouette against the gray winter sky. It was the highest building in town, here in a place of low-lying garages, sparkling new banks to take advantage of the refugees from Hurricane Katrina, and old ramshackle wooden buildings between run-down strip malls. The road ended a few blocks later at Lee's old stomping ground, the Azalea Rest Cemetery. In Zachary the difference between life and death was a mere matter of blocks.

Across the street from the cemetery was Sammy's Grill. It was Friday night. Inside, Sammy's was a rowdy family place. Half of the men wore silver belt buckles and boots. A few had on white Stetsons. All of them were Louisiana State University Tigers fans. To be anything less would court murder.

There was a small bar in the front. The rest of the large room was taken up by table after table of families eating heaping big portions of fried food. Patting my Lipitor bottle in my right hip pocket for confidence, I strolled over to the bar to try and unclog my arteries.

"Southern Comfort Manhattan," I said to the girl behind the bar.

She blinked. "If you tell me what's in it, I can make it," she said with a practiced honeyed voice.

When I told her, she said she was out of sweet vermouth.

"How about a vodka gimlet?"

She blinked.

"Rose's lime juice and vodka."

Her face lit up. "I can do that. What kind of vodka?"

She had me there.

While she got my drink, the African-American woman on the stool next to me, a broad-shouldered girl with corn rows, looked up with brown eyes through a haze of smoke.

"You got your drink, I see," she said, exhaling from her Marlboro as the bartender put a perfectly mixed gimlet in front of me. I sipped it, and gave her the thumbs-up. She said her name was Kimberly.

"You old enough to smoke?" I asked.

"How old you think I look?"

"Seventeen," I lied.

"Shoot," she said laughing, "I'm twenty-one. I guess you could say I was experienced," she added, chuckling.

She asked me what I was doing there.

"I'm meeting the girl who survived the Baton Rouge Serial Killer, Derrick Todd Lee."

"I know Derrick Lee," said the twenty-one-year-old Kimberly nonchalantly, smiling and puffing on her Marlboro. "I grew up with Derrick. He was in my town where I grew up. He was a ladies' man."

She smiled.

"He ever bother you?"

Kimberly shook her head with a look that said the guy wouldn't dare.

Just then, Michele Whitehead walked in the door. She wasn't a fifteen-year-old girl any longer, but a twenty-eight-year-old woman, the former Michele Chapman, married now eight years. Petite, about five feet nothing and maybe 116 pounds soaking wet, Michele had a pretty face with a little too much makeup. Her full lips were redder than they needed to be. It was her dark eyes that were truly beautiful.

She had come with her mother, Roberta, who wore a black skirt and top tailored to slim her weight down. When I turned to introduce them to Kimberly, she was gone.

"We thought you might want some good Creole cooking," Roberta said as we sat at a table by a big plate-glass window with SAMMY'S spelled out in red and green neon.

"I love Creole cooking," I answered truthfully. I'd had a delicious dish called Shrimp Creole Agnew in New Orleans when I was a teenager. They called it something else after 1974.

Michele was quiet, smiling, talking to the waitress, a girl she had known since grade school. Just then, Roberta looked up and spotted her husband Ron sauntering along the concrete walkway outside the restaurant.

"There he is," she said balefully.

Michele got tense. She looked up as her dad came through the door.

The only way to describe Ron Chapman is to say he is a presence. That night, his massive torso was draped in a well-fitted American flag shirt. Ron's a decorated Vietnam vet, the kind of smart, small-town guy who fought and suffered, whose government abandoned him with old war wounds both psychic and physical.

Ron introduced himself as Michele's father. He shook my hand with a massive paw that substituted for a hand. As soon as he sat, a smiling waitress came over to take his drink order.

"I'll have a Jack an' a Jack an' a Bud Light," he said to the waitress.

"Don't you mean a double Jack Daniel's?" I asked.

"No, it's a Jack an' a Jack an' a Bud Light," said Ron with a cagey smile.

"Which way is Oak Shadows?" I asked the waitress, who used to babysit Michele and wasn't much older herself.

"Just a little down the road that way," she answered. "Just a few blocks east."

So that's where Connie Warner lived, I thought. Connie Warner was a forty-one-year-old divorcée who lived in the Oak Shadows neighborhood of Zachary with her teenager, Sally. On April 23, 1992, at about 9:00 A.M., when Sally Warner arrived home after a weekend of partying, she couldn't find her mom. Expecting her mother to be home, she was puzzled when she didn't answer her shouts. Her mom had bad night vision. She rarely ventured out past dark.

Three hours later she still hadn't showed. Sally

was frantic. She called her grandfather, who came over immediately. Searching the house together for some clue as to Connie's disappearance, they found one—blood spatter. Immediately, they called the police.

When Lieutenant David McDavid of the three-man Zachary detective bureau got to the scene, he looked at the home's perimeter, locks, and windows for any sign of forced entry. There was none. Inside the house, in Connie's bedroom, the bed-clothes were mussed up; and furniture had been overturned. You didn't have to be Nero Wolfe, or Archie Goodwin for that matter, to figure out that these were clear signs of a struggle between Warner and her attacker. The blood spatter the daughter and grandfather found just confirmed it.

McDavid was baffled. How had the killer gained entry to the home? If he hadn't broken in, then Warner opened the door to him. A search by forensic technicians of Warner's car found evidence that her abductor had driven her car to Baton Rouge. Then, he had apparently turned around and driven back, leaving the car in the carport, like it had never been used.

Except to drop off a body, of course. That was confirmed two weeks later when a truck driver found Warner's body in a ditch near a Baton Rouge area lake. Naked, decomposing, the medical examiner's report would attribute death due to strangulation; there were ligature marks on her neck.

A check of acquaintances showed that Connie

Warner had no known enemies and no disgruntled family members. Then the killer must have been a stranger, McDavid theorized.

That was unfortunate; it would make him harder to find. Much harder. Cops hate stranger-on-stranger crime for that reason. Fact is, they rely on probability to get their killers. And the probability in most cases of homicide was that in some way the deceased knew their murderer.

Murder for money, revenge, sex, drugs, and any legitimate motive can usually be tied to some sort of a relationship between the dead person and their killer. But stranger-on-stranger is a motiveless crime, unless looked at in the abstract. Even a sophisticated big city police force has trouble with serial killing cases for this reason, let alone a three-person detective force like Zachary's.

The waitress brought over our drinks. As Ron Chapman began work on his first Jack, his daughter Michele remembered that April 3, 1993, was a warm day and a warm night in Zachary. By night, the thunderstorms had moved in and it was raining.

"I was a student at Zachary High School, a senior majoring in journalism. I was a pretty good gymnast, I wasn't going to the Olympics or anything, but I had a good shot at a gymnastics scholarship to LSU in Baton Rouge. Most of the local kids go there, if they go to college at all."

Michele was dating Ricky Johnson.

"Ricky had a 1992 Toyota Corolla, burgundy,

with a maroon interior. We drove over to the cemetery to make out."

"The Azalea Rest Cemetery across the street?"

Michele nodded. "We were in the backseat making out. Then this guy comes out of nowhere and opens the passenger side door in the backseat," she continued. "It was happening so fast . . . he was hacking away with something. Ricky jumped in my way, shouting—"

"Ricky saved her life!" Ron Chapman suddenly shouted, and then repeated, "Ricky saved her life!"

"Dad, stop . . ." Exasperated, Michele looked over at her father. "You finished?" she asked gently.

"I'm finished," Ron replied, reaching for the second Jack.

"When Ricky got in his way, I crawled over the front seat and tried to start the car," Michele continued.

About two blocks away, Officer Bob Eubanks of the Zachary Police Department stopped his police cruiser at the intersection of the Dunkin' Donuts and Blockbuster video. In the distance, in the cemetery, he saw a light, and shadows passing in front of it.

When the "guy" had opened the car door, the dome light came on automatically. What Eubanks was seeing, but didn't know it yet, was the life and death battle taking place inside the car between fifteen-year-old Michele Chapman and her unknown assailant.

Michele had made it into the front seat. In the back, Ricky was trying to hold back the "bad guy," to no avail. Michele had just seated herself behind the wheel, her foot barely touching the pedals, when she looked back. He had escaped Ricky's grasp and was jumping into the front seat.

"He was dressed really nice," Michele recalled. "Wearing a red plaid shirt tucked in. Buttoned up. I could see the rage in his wiggly, bloodshot eyes. He came after me. We fought for the keys. They were still in the ignition. Finally, he pulled 'em out and ran off. Ricky was trying to get out of his way. Ricky jumped over me, trying to close the door after the guy."

Eubanks had followed up his hunch and driven into the cemetery. He saw something flit in front of his headlights for a second. Then, it was gone. He drove down a narrow road in the cemetery, passing gravestones. Then his lights lit up the Toyota and the bloodied faces inside.

"I didn't feel anything but I was smelling blood," Michele said. "There was blood everywhere. My ankle was severed, the nerve above the ankle twice. Severe pain. I didn't . . . I was hysterical. I sure wasn't . . . I lost movement."

On the ground nearby, the cop found a bloody sword cane. The cane part was merely a crude wooden sheath. But the blade was sharp. Someone had made certain of that. It had sliced through flesh like butter.

"He must have been in the neighborhood. Otherwise, how could he find us in the cemetery so fast?" Michele continued. But she had more important things to worry about in the aftermath of her assault.

" 'Where's Ricky? Where's Ricky?' I kept screaming when I got to Lane Memorial Hospital, which is nearby. I was so concerned about him. Then this assistant district attorney comes over to talk to me. He's telephoning . . . my dad finally arrived . . ."

"You know what happened? Know what happened?" Ron's voice rose. "I had a friend get me out of a meeting and tell me my daughter was at the hospital and someone had attacked her. I ran over there so fast . . ."

Michele exhaled deeply and looked at her father, not with anger, not with shame, but strangely, with pity.

"Sorry," said Ron sheepishly.

"It would take me over a year of physical therapy to regain feeling," Michele continued. "I was going to be a teacher but that had to be postponed." She continued to see Ricky. "I was pregnant a year and a half later with Ricky's child."

During that time, Derrick Todd Lee was in and out of jail on a variety of burglary charges. Everyone who came in contact with him found him not only agreeable, but charming. He could charm the pants off anyone, so why did he insist on tearing them off?

"We knew Randi Mebruer before she disappeared," said Ron, taking a swig of his second Bud Light. "We knew her."

Randi Mebruer turned up missing on April 19, 1998. Once again, it was in the same Oak Shadows neighborhood, within blocks of the Warner murder site. While her three-year-old son Michael slept in a nearby room down the hall, Mebruer was kidnapped literally out of her sleep. "Attacked" was actually a better description. The Mebruer hallway was streaked with what forensics would soon determine was Mebruer's own blood. McDavid figured they fought in the bedroom and he got the better of her. Then he dragged her down the hallway. Confirming that theory, McDavid discovered Randi's contact lenses lying next to each other farther down the hallway, just inches apart. Randi had apparently been facedown when she was hit hard enough to dislodge both lenses at the same time.

Downstairs there was blood spatter from the kitchen to the carport. Her assailant had dragged the body outside for transportation to a dump site. Searching the carport, forensics eyed a pink plastic roll of garbage bags. On the outside of the plastic roll, standing out against the pink background, was a spot of blood and a spot of what would later be identified as semen.

All police attempts to locate Randi Mebruer came up empty. She had apparently disappeared off the face of the earth, or perhaps into it.

McDavid became certain that whoever had hurt

and probably killed Mebruer was the same guy who had murdered Connie Warner.

. Randi Mebruer's body has never been found.

"She's under concrete," said Roberta matter-of-factly. Michele and her father nodded.

After *America's Most Wanted* aired a 1998 re-enactment of Chapman's case, McDavid began to suspect that her case was tied in with the two murders. It was the same guy.

"I had done a first sketch for McDavid, in which it looked like Eubanks. Then McDavid heard the stories about Lee being a Peeping Tom and burglar. He favored Oak Shadows," said Michele.

McDavid connected the dots.

"McDavid called and asked me to come in for a photo lineup. There was this big album. There were three people. I pointed right at him. McDavid jumped up and down, he was so excited."

"That's Derrick Todd Lee!" McDavid had shouted.

It was February 1999, with only six weeks to go on the statute of limitations for the attempted murder of Michele Chapman. It was the only crime that Lee could possibly be charged with. The Zachary District Attorney's Office then made the crucial decision not to prosecute for the Chapman attempted murder because the assault weapon—the sword cane, which was the crucial bit of forensic evidence—had been dropped in the rain, washing it free of fingerprints. All they had to rely on was Chapman's ID, and they didn't feel it was enough.

"It was more than frustrating," Michele said, her voice finally rising in anger. "They knew who the guy was and they couldn't get him? Come on!"

"We're not big McDavid fans either," said Ron.

He grabbed for a Jack. The waitress came over with another one. Ron's gaze had turned glassy.

It was easy to understand why they were so angry. The problem was, no one was *listening*. Derrick Todd Lee had presented as classic a case of "serial killeritis" as any in American criminal history. Lee was literally working his way up to a serial killing spree.

All the classic signs criminologists write about were there. Lee was a guy who as a boy—a *boy!*—was a Peeping Tom with sadomasochistic fantasies. As an adult, he had an extensive record as a burglar, another crime on many a serial killer's resume. Lee had also continued his nocturnal Peeping Tom activities and occasionally perpetrated strong-arm assaults against his various lovers.

Why wasn't a red flag put on his behavior? The answer is: knowledge and resources. What criminologists in New York know, for example, is not necessarily what a poor social worker or cop knows in a rural section of an impoverished state like Louisiana.

Then, the bodies really started really piling up.

The first was Gina Green. Her death didn't get any press outside of Louisiana. She was killed on

September 24, 2001, thirteen days after the Al Qaeda attack on the World Trade Center. A pretty forty-two-year-old nurse, Green was found strangled inside her home on Stanford Avenue, a nice tree-lined neighborhood near LSU. Amid the continual media hoopla of showing the attacks over and over on TV, there was precious little time or resources to devote to an obscure murder in a small southern town of one woman . . . or so they thought.

There were no leads to the perpetrator.

"By January, 2002, I had enrolled in LSU," Michelle Whitehead recalled. "It had taken me a year of physical therapy to get movement back to my ankle. It was really very hard and painful to come back that far, but I did it. I joined the National Honors Society with a 3.9 GPA."

Ricky Johnson was doing much worse. He never talked about what happened. Despite now being a man in his mid-twenties, he still lived at home. They had split up long ago, but still had something together. Theirs was truly a love child, born from survivors of as brutal a serial killer as any that had come down the proverbial pike.

Michele still bore the physical and especially emotional scars of the assault. Her attack left her with an irrational fear of being alone in a room with a black man. It was something she could feel. Sometimes, if she let her mind wander when her route to LSU took her over the bridge spanning Interstate 10, she would flash back to that moment when she looked into the eyes of the man she now knew was Derrick Todd Lee.

That bridge over Interstate 10 is a tangled, rusting monstrosity that arches over the Mississippi River. On the other side of the river, in a trailer parked off a secluded stretch of Louisiana Highway 1, Geralyn DeSoto fought for her life. The way police later reconstructed it was like this:

On January 14, 2002, DeSoto was getting ready for a 2:30 P.M. interview for a job as an occupational therapist. Before noon, someone broke into her mobile home. Grabbing the telephone, he hit her in the head with it. Then he pulled some sort of knife and stabbed DeSoto three times. DeSoto summoned all her strength to run in her bedroom. She had a shotgun.

But she wasn't fast enough.

The "bad guy" pulled the gun, barrel first, out of her small hands. Eschewing the weapon's immediate and perhaps impersonal method of killing, he used his knife to carefully slice DeSoto's throat from ear to ear. As she lay on the floor bleeding out, her lifeless eyes looked up as her killer stomped them back in her head.

By this time the Baton Rouge police had finally added up two and two, and amazingly, the product was four. They correctly deduced that they had a serial killer in their midst. Any lingering doubts were put to rest on May 31, 2002, when Charlotte Murray Pace, twenty-one years old, was found in her south Baton Rouge home.

Seasoned homicide investigators were repelled by the bloody crime scene, which was right out of Jack the Ripper. Pace had been stabbed eighty-two times. Her throat had been cut ear to ear. The final indignity to Pace's body was being beaten with a clothes iron.

Then, as if in Pace's honor, before police even had the results of their forensic tests back, the serial killer stepped up *his* pace. Four weeks later, in early July 2002, Pamela R. Kinamore, a pretty brunette, went missing from her Baton Rouge home. Four days later her body was discovered floating in Whiskey Bay, thirty miles away from her home. Her throat had been slashed. Police theorized her body was dumped off Interstate 10 between Baton Rouge and Lafayette.

A few days afterward, the Baton Rouge cops told David McDavid not to let the door hit him in the ass on the way out.

Things had started out politely, with the Baton Rouge Police Department conducting a meeting of detectives gathered from the city's surrounding communities. The idea was to exchange information about cases that might be linked to the guy the press had now dubbed the "Baton Rouge Serial Killer." He seemed to be feeding on women in the prime of life.

McDavid, who by that time had gotten Louisiana State Attorney General's Investigator Dannie

Mixon assigned to the Zachary cases, informed the "big city" Baton Rouge cops that they had a prime suspect: African-American Derrick Todd Lee. McDavid told the detectives present of three Zachary cases he was certain were linked to the Baton Rouge homicides: the murder of Connie Warner, the abduction and probable murder of the missing Randi Mebruer, and the attempted murder of Michele Chapman.

The big shots told the small town cop that the FBI had come in with one of their profiles and, by gum, it had to be right, because it was the FBI! The FBI said the serial killer was a white man. Lee was black. End of story. Showing the kind of stupidity even a memoir writer can't make up, on that basis alone the Baton Rouge Task Force (BRTF) eliminated Lee as a suspect.

Don't let the door hit you on the way out boys . . . and McDavid and Dannie Mixon went back to Zachary, more certain than ever that they had the right guy.

In this case, and others, blatant racism built into the FBI response to a serial killer running amuck means that African Americans are deliberately excluded from the list of suspects simply because of their skin color. It is a perverse form of racism that sees crime, literally, as black and white, and concludes that blacks aren't smart enough to be serial killers. Somewhere, J. Edgar Hoover must have been smiling.

Ironically, it was because of this bias that an

African-American woman, Treneisha Dene Colomb, had to die. While the Baton Rouge Task
Force was busy taking DNA samples from any
foolish white suspects who would consent, the real
guy—a black man who Michele Whitehead,
McDavid, and Mixon knew had to be Derrick
Todd Lee—outdid himself.

Colomb was visiting her mother's grave in St.
Landry Parish on November 21, 2002, when she
disappeared. Her car was found nearby. Apparently, the killer had stalked her into the cemetery
and robbed her from one grave to put her in another. Three days later her body was discovered
dumped in the woods about twenty miles away.
She was beaten to death, and semen at the scene
positively linked her killer to the murders of Gina
Wilson Green, Charlotte Murray Pace, and Pam
Kinamore. It was the same guy.

The women of Baton Rouge were terrified they
would be the next victim of the Baton Rouge Serial Killer. Sales of knives, guns, Mace, and pepper
sprays went sky high. The media stoked it, but the
panic was real. The serial killer appeared and disappeared at will. The task force's racial blindness
continued, as more and more white suspects were
pulled into their DNA dragnet.

Carrie Lynn Yoder was unloading some grocer-
ies from her car on March 3, 2003, when someone
snatched her. A graduate of LSU, which is as common in Baton Rouge as chewing tobacco, Yoder
lived just south of the campus. Her body was found

ten days later floating in Whiskey Bay, a mere mile and a half from where Kinamore had also been found, out for her morning float.

The M.E.'s report stated that the cause of death was strangulation. However, the method of death also included a severe beating. Someone had hit Yoder so hard, her liver was lacerated and her ribs shattered. She had also been raped. Once again the semen the killer left at the scene was linked to all the previous Baton Rouge murders.

A few months later, in May 2003, "I graduated from LSU, twenty-fifth in a class of 225," Michele Whitehead said with pride.

At the same time she was graduating from LSU, up in Zachary, the state attorney general's investigator, Dannie Mixon, had just about had it. He decided to work up a paper time line on their prime suspect, Derrick Todd Lee. Looking down at his paper trail, Mixon saw that Lee had spent a lot of time over the last decade going in and out of jail on low level felonies and misdemeanors.

And every time he was out of custody, every single one of the murders in Zachary and Baton Rouge—and the attempted murder of Michele Chapman—occurred.

With a DNA sample from Lee, the deaths could finally be put to rest. But obtaining DNA from a suspect is not easy. It is the same as serving a search warrant. You need what a court calls "proper cause" to serve the warrant, which allows you to violate the individual's person and collect the DNA sample.

By showing his time line and comparison to the crimes, the ongoing murder investigation by Zachary detectives with Lee as prime suspect, and, more important to the public profile of the case, the murders in the big city of Baton Rouge, Mixon hoped a judge would see it his way. He wrote a six-page application for a search warrant and sought out a judge in East Feliciana Parish. Replying to the application, the judge issued a subpoena *duces tecum*: a court order that allowed Mixon to take a DNA swab from Derrick Todd Lee.

Mixon personally got Lee to give him a DNA swab from his mouth without a struggle. When the results came back on May 25, 2003, Lee's DNA matched the DNA found at all the crime scenes. Dannie Mixon had solved the case. Derrick Todd Lee was the Baton Rouge Serial Killer.

He was also gone.

Once they took his DNA, Lee knew the cops had him. He went on the run and was caught a few days later in Georgia, hiding out at a trailer park where he was the king of the barbecues. He was then extradited back to Louisiana to stand trial.

Chief Pat Englade of the Baton Rouge Police Department took much of the credit for Lee's identification as the killer and his subsequent arrest after a fugitive flight to Georgia. He later said he planned to write a true crime book about the case. He neglected to explain why at least one person died at Lee's hands who didn't have to.

FBI Special Agent Charles Cunningham told

CNN, "What will happen now is we'll try to identify every city, every place that this individual has been. Try to link any unsolved murders that may have been accomplished by this individual agent."

*T*he transcript of the task force cops' interview with Lee, which included the presence of a senior FBI agent, tells a different story.

Derrick Todd Lee had more charm and guile than all of his interrogators put together. He kept the inept task force cops busy for hours with a nonstatement statement. Most of it consisted of investigators pleading with Lee to confess. It resembled a hip-hop version of an old Warner Bros. 1930s gangster movie where, typically, Pat O'Brien implores Jimmy Cagney to confess for the good of the kids, blah blah blah.

The Millennium twist was that the cops were asking the killer to confess because they had him dead to rights on the DNA that he left inside his victims when he raped them. The confession would be the icing on the cake. The highlight of the interview was the following introduction by the Baton Rouge cop who was interrogating Lee:

"Derrick Todd Lee, this is Mary Ellen O'Toole," said Chris Jenkins.

Dr. Mary Ellen O'Toole, Ph.D., came into the interrogation room.

"I feel like I know you, Derrick," she said.

"Ma'am."

Serial killers can be polite just like other people. "I've studied you for a long time."

It struck a sympathetic note. O'Toole introduced herself as the supervisory special agent of the FBI's Behavioral Analysis Unit, in Quantico, Virginia.

"Our unit is the Profile Unit at the FBI Academy. Are you familiar with FBI profilers?"

"No ma'am, no more than what he told me."

Lee had a thought.

"Maybe somebody out there may want one day to come to you to make a movie. Chris not even gonna be in it because he's the detective. Your name gonna be in there because you the profiler."

Derrick Todd Lee, a man of his time.

*O*n August 10, 2004, Derrick Todd Lee was found guilty of the second degree murder of Geralyn DeSoto and sentenced to life imprisonment, the most the statute allowed. However, he wasn't so lucky during his second trial.

On October 12, 2004, Lee was found guilty of the first degree murder of Charlotte Murray Pace. His defense attorneys had rested without calling a single witness. They thought the state had not proven its case beyond a reasonable doubt. Three days later the Pace jury took only ninety minutes at the end of the penalty phase of the trial to recommend a sentence of death. Rather than accept experts for the defense who asserted during the hearing that Lee was mentally retarded—which would mean he could not be executed—the jury believed otherwise.

Lee still has to stand trial for the rest of the murders in Baton Rouge and Zachary. Prosecutors in Lafayette Parish, where Lee killed Trineisha Dene Colomb, declined to take the case to trial. They felt that the Colomb family did not need to be put through a trial, especially since Lee already had one death sentence against him. How many times could the state execute one man? However, the parish reserved the right to prosecute if an appeals court ever overturned Lee's death sentence.

It was 9:30 in Zachary and they were rolling up the sidewalks. Inside Sammy's, Michele Whitehead, Ron and Roberta Chapman, and I were the last ones left.

"I want to meet him," Michele Whitehead said suddenly. "Derrick Lee, I want to meet him. See what makes him tick. When I was in school, I minored in criminal justice."

"Did you figure out what makes serial killers tick?"

She shook her head.

"Why didn't you die that night?" I asked.

"I believe he [God] said it wasn't time yet, for some reason. I think he had something else for me in mind."

"Like being a wife and mother?"

She smiled.

"Did you ever wonder why you fought back?"

"What do you mean?"

"Lots of people who get attacked by serial killers don't fight back."

"Why not?"

While Michele Whitehead had accepted what happened to her, her father had not. After his Jacks and beers, the alcohol broke down Ron's bluff exterior. Ron Chapman shook, the grief engulfing him, and he buried his head in his hands. I understood: he couldn't protect his daughter.

"My husband hasn't gotten drunk like that in four years, you have to excuse him," said Roberta when we got outside.

"Why? He has every right in the world to feel the way he does. The country that he fought and lost for let him down."

"But he hasn't come to terms with it, with what happened to *me*," said Michele.

"And he has to do that himself," Roberta added.

"He's not driving?" I asked.

"He's not driving," Roberta confirmed, shaking her head and giving her husband a glance filled with love, and with pity. She had worked her way through the pain. So had the other victim, their daughter Michele. Now it was Ron's turn.

"I'll take him back," Roberta told her daughter.

My car was in the shadows. As I walked toward it, I looked back to see Ron, composed now, chatting up a few of the good ol' boys outside Sammy's. The Stetsons rode high and the belt buckles shined. And there was Ron, draped in the symbol of the country he had fought and bled for, that had clearly let him down. That, perhaps, was the worst of it.

Making a left onto the boulevard of angels, I passed in front of the cemetery where Michele's life was saved by her frantic fight to stay alive, Ricky's intervention, and, most of all, the headlights of Bob Eubanks's car. Mine picked their way a little bit more surely through the canebrake, back to the interstate.

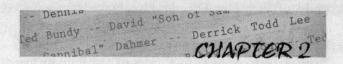
Survivor: Kevin Bright
Serial Killer: Dennis Rader aka "BTK"

"I can't stop it . . . it controls me, you know, it's like in the driver's seat. That's probably the reason we're sitting here. You know, if I could just say, 'No, I don't want to do this,' and go crawl into a hole, but it's driving me."
—Dennis Rader

*H*eading west out of Baton Rouge, Interstate 10 becomes a series of viaducts over the swamps of southern Louisiana. Thousands of thick tree limbs break the water's brackish surface. In the late morning light they looked like razor-sharp brown scimitars.

The swamp's warm waters were home to alligators and other natural predators. Between the *Jurassic Park* throwbacks and the high water temperature, a body dumped in the swamps would literally disintegrate to sludge in days. More than one killer had thought the same thing. It really did seem like a strange place to put an interstate.

The interstate highway system was the brainchild of President Dwight Eisenhower. Ike envisioned and commissioned it during his tenure as president. His idea was to connect the country from coast to coast with a series of overlapping interstate super highways like Germany's Autobahn. Ike had seen the Autobahn when he visited Germany after World War I and decided that America should have a similar transportation system. When he had his opportunity to give it to the country, he did.

As in the past, the first travelers over the new roads were the criminals looking to scam, thieve, rob, and murder. For serial killers, Eisenhower provided an unknowing bonanza. Like everyone else, they could now move quickly on newly paved, high-speed highways, preying on people in larger kill zones than ever before. They even had a choice of which of three, coast-to-coast interstates to terrorize: Interstates 80, 90, or 10.

Serving the southern part of the continental United States, Interstate 10 connects the country from Santa Monica and Los Angeles in the west to Jacksonville in the east. The highway passes through every major city across the Southwest and South, including Phoenix, El Paso, San Antonio, Houston, Baton Rouge, and New Orleans. I traveled much of the western section in the 1970s and early 1980s, when it was still a little used highway instead of the freeway it has become today.

Before Katrina, Interstate 10's busyness provided exceptional anonymity. Prostitutes, drug addicts, and hitchhikers who congregate at the truck stops along the way are the kind of victims serial killers like—those with erratic work hours who will not be missed. Add to the mix single women traveling in their cars alone, and teenagers out for some kicks, and it is understandable why the vulnerable become their prey.

With over a million people displaced by the hurricane throughout the South, Interstate 10 in southern Louisiana and eastern Texas in late December 2005 was a seemingly endless parade of trailers, cars, and trucks. It only served to make an active, anonymous highway that much busier, that much more anonymous, that much more loaded with potential victims. Driving along behind a semi at 75, it's hard to pay attention to the dude raping the girl in the car by the side of the road and then dumping her body to disintegrate in the swamp.

Going west, Interstate 10 passed into Texas over the Sabine River. Almost immediately the landscape changed. The swamp dried up and evergreens dotted the highway. Texas seemed drier, not to mention friendlier. Considering the ongoing trauma in Louisiana, the stark contrast was more than understandable. It was a relief to finally leave the interstate behind and turn north onto Highway 287 and then onto U.S. 190 heading west. Almost immediately, federal law was left behind.

The Alabama and Coushatta Indian Reservation

occupies 4,600 timber-rich acres directly east of Livingston, Texas. Except for the birds, the silence was startling. The reservation is the home of the Alabama and Coushatta tribes, former members of the Creek Confederacy. Hailing from Alabama and Mississippi, they had allied themselves with the French in pre-Colonial times.

The French defeat at the hands of the colonial English—what became known as the French-Indian War—meant the Alabama and Coushatta had also been defeated. Rather than stay under English law, which to them represented a form of slavery, the two tribes picked up and left. By the time David ("Don't call me Davy") Crockett, Sam Houston, and former slave trader Jim Bowie arrived in the future state, the Alabama and Coushatta had already settled in East Texas, where their reservation is today.

One of the prime sources of revenue for the tribe was their "trading post," set up on the highway where you could buy Native American crafts, jewelry, and all kinds of Alabama and Coushatta tchochkes. The reservation trading post sold a purple dream catcher with a label that said "Made in Malaysia." It was comforting to know that the tribes had done well enough over the years to outsource their labors.

The last ten miles into Livingston were driven in fading afternoon light. By the time the headlights picked out a battered black on white sign that said LIVINGSTON, it was near the end of what filmmakers call the "magic hour," directly before dark when everything takes on a blue, almost otherworldly glow and feeling.

Livingston was a desolate place of weathered wooden buildings from the nineteenth century alongside worn brick buildings from the early twentieth. The town's storefronts were mostly vacant. This was a poor town at Christmastime, with its best days far behind. The Wal-Mart in the middle of town was the only building that looked prosperous. Lit up like a blue spruce in green and red holiday lights, Wal-Mart beckoned shoppers with its ripe delights, and at a good price.

Inside, the shoppers seemed a cheerful bunch despite the fact that most of them were paying on credit, and at the usurious rates the credit card companies are allowed to charge. Scanning the registers, the fellow manning register four clearly stood out from the rest.

He wasn't a local and didn't even try to hide it. He has a hauntingly pale face and the chiseled features of a Kansas frontiersman, not too surprising since he is a Kansas native. Pale blue eyes that searched right through you, and prematurely white hair combed neatly to the side, made it hard to pin down his age. Wiry at about five-six and 140 pounds, he looked like a pushover.

"Kevin Bright?" I asked, extending my hand.

He shook it warmly, keeping a careful eye on the young mother's sack he was filling while ringing her up. She was the archetypal, multitasking mom, baby plastered to her right hip, cell phone to her left ear. Being informed, the multitasking mom would certainly have heard of BTK. The reason it would have been relevant to her, though, was that the man waiting on her was the only survivor of BTK, and the only one Dennis Rader could not kill.

"I'll be off the register as soon as I'm relieved," Kevin explained.

Waiting for Bright to finish his shift, I sat on a bench in the front of the store. Suddenly, the tubercular Marlboro Man sat down next to me. He had the sweet stink of Jim Beam. His goatee had wilted and hung down like a limp, half-eaten Thai noodle. Leaning back against the slats, his gaunt face composed itself into so many leathery wrinkles. He looked like what used to be called a "lunger."

"It's all about reading the signs and symbols," the tubercular Marlboro Man said gravely, looking seriously at me with intense black eyes. That made sense.

One thing about Rader—he definitely left lots of signs and symbols. The problem was the lack of people experienced enough to read and interpret them.

Saturday, February 26, 2005

The rising CNN star and soon-to-be anchor Anderson Cooper was screaming something about the

BTK Serial Killer. In between the hyperbole, he finally said the word "caught!"

BTK is the only active serial killer in American criminal history who remained at large for three decades while he continued to kill as police actively hunted him. During that time period, from 1976 to 2005, BTK frequently stopped his killing activities. Those times, he was dormant evil waiting for the inevitable eruption. Wichita police stumbled around like a sighted person in the dark, powerless to see where he was.

They were constantly being outsmarted by the "bad guy." They couldn't find him. It wasn't the cops' fault . . . really. Their reliance on the vaunted FBI Behavioral Science Unit, which claimed they accurately profiled serial killers, doomed their investigation from the start. The Feds advice, as in all such cases, was absolutely worthless. That meant it would take a serious mistake by BTK to catch him.

The self-described Bondage Torture Killer—BTK for short—had taunted police in letter after letter. While that kind of written contact between cop and serial killer seems clichéd now, with the glut of serial killer fiction and film on the market, it was BTK who popularized it in the last third of the twentieth century.

The cops eventually backtracked those notes to their sources in 2005. The serial killer's unchecked ego had finally gotten him. After a serial killing spree of thirty-one years, "the man suspected in a string of ten slayings attributed to the BTK serial killer confessed to at least six of those killings," said Anderson Cooper.

Through the killer's own confession and DNA evidence, BTK had finally been identified as fifty-nine-year-old Dennis Rader. As the case progressed and Wichita police released more information about Rader, it turned out that like most sociopaths, he hid in plain sight. What is fascinating about Rader, though, is how far off the chart he is in his overall behavior. Like Jeffrey Dahmer, Rader defies categorization by the very nature and extent of his psychopathy.

Dennis Rader is the Millennium's only serial killer to have a marksman's badge from the United States Air Force and two academic degrees from respected colleges. With that kind of intelligence, backed up by the instincts of an Army-trained killer, it is no wonder he remained at large for so long free to kill.

Cops, reporters, lawyers, everyone who subsequently came in contact with him, all said the same thing: "Rader's a real prick! He's got an ego the size of the Empire State Building." As strange as it sounds, not all serial killers are loathsome people. Some are able to imitate pleasant personalities even after incarceration. Rader inspired a new level of pure hatred even among hardened cops.

Rader spent four years in the Air Force, from 1966 to 1970. Trained as a small arms expert, he shot for a marksman's badge. After his discharge, the Kansas native returned home and married Paula E. Dietz in 1971. The same year, he entered Butler County Community College in El Dorado. He graduated in May 1973 with an Associate's Degree in Electronics.

In 1975 the happy couple had their first child, Brian Howard, and then a daughter, Kerri Lynn, in 1978. By all accounts a loving and supportive father and husband, Rader aspired to higher things. In 1973, he entered Wichita State University, graduating in 1979 with a Bachelor of Science degree in Administrative Justice. He may be the only serial killer in U.S. history so credentialed.

A Boy and Cub Scouts leader for twenty years, a registered Republican who was tough on crime, he finally conned his way into the best "cover" a serial killer could have. From January 2005 until his arrest that March, Rader was the president of Wichita's Christ Lutheran Church. He had been a member for three decades.

By day, Dennis Rader put his bachelor's degree to work. He was Code Enforcement Supervisor for Park City, a Wichita suburb. In charge of animal control, nuisances, inoperable vehicles, and general code compliance, Rader's position brought him in regular contact with the public. He even got on the local news. In 2001, Dennis Rader did a TV spot, in uniform, for a report on vicious dogs running wild in Park City. It may be the only TV spot ever done by a serial killer in broadcast history.

In addition to his obvious social, religious, and economic accomplishments, Rader had previously worked for home security companies, where he became expert at home security systems and penetrating them. He was getting on-the-job serial killer training. A meticulous sort, he would draw detailed plans of customer's houses, then double-check to make sure that the technicians he supervised installed systems correctly.

When he was finally caught, the reaction of this local hero's friends and family to his arrest as the notorious BTK was "disbelief, absolute disbelief," said Carole Nelson, a member of Christ Lutheran Church. "I never would have guessed in a million years."

According to Michael Clark, the family's pastor, when he visited the Rader family after their paterfamilias's arrest, he found Paula Rader in a state of total shock. "Her demeanor and voice indicated she was suffering," Clark said.

That made sense. It would turn out she had no idea what Rader had done because he'd kept that dark side of his life a total secret to his family and friends. Sociopaths can do that. Everything is a pose. They are like chameleons that absorb the surroundings. Unfortunately, they are also capable of absorbing life force by taking it in the most extreme cases.

*T*he tubercular Marlboro Man had vanished. Standing near the registers, I gazed at a guy across the aisle whose beard was about as long as the twenty-seven-inch TV he was cradling in his arms. He held it like it weighed only as much as a sack of potatoes.

"Look at their *teeth*," said the tall, thin woman who suddenly appeared at my elbow. "First thing we noticed when we got here is all these people with teeth missing, and some of them, they're rotten."

I smiled, and then thought better of it. I didn't know her, but she thought I should. She caught my "Who are you?" expression.

"Oh, I'm sorry, I'm Kevin's wife, Sharon."

She extended a hard flat hand and we shook. Sharon wore little red Christmas bells on her white sneakers. Somehow, she made them look good.

"You know, you're right. About the teeth," I answered. "That's probably because they don't have money for proper care, insurance, or both."

Kevin came out from behind his register. As cashiers, both he and Sharon were dressed exactly the same—white top and black pants. She looked slightly taller. Then I saw that the other three cashiers were also standing out in the aisle, again all dressed in the same uniforms. It was a Wal-Mart thing, to entice customers. But none of them really wanted to ring up any sales. It was close to 6:30 P.M. and the shift should have already ended.

They had all been on their feet for eight or more hours and wanted to knock off for the night. Kevin and Sharon were particularly anxious to leave. We all stood tall, alert and at attention like automatons, waiting for the next customer but really waiting for the damn relief to show up.

Tuesday, June 28, 2005

From start to finish, the criminal case against Dennis Rader took four months to the day. It is a model of the legal profession, of what can happen when a state chooses to seek justice rather than vengeance.

During that brief time, CNN fought Fox News tooth and nail to see who could deliver the most exhaustive coverage of the case. Likewise, all the country's tabloids and even the more respected broadsheets, including the *New York Times* and the *Washington Post,* vied to break stories that would shed new light on the case.

The families of the victims were paraded out for the media to interrogate. They turned out to be victims too. Most were interviewed on live satellite feed. They sat in some small TV studio near their hometown, with klieg lights shining in their faces, facing sleek robot-controlled cameras on live television. With so-called anchors shouting questions in their ears, they were expected to deliver reasonable, plausible, and, perhaps most important for ratings, emotional answers.

Instead, what frequently happened was that because of the interviewees' unfamiliarity with modern telemetry, they did not hear—or they misunderstood—questions shouted at them through their audio devices. The resulting answers were often totally irrelevant; the anchors didn't seem to care.

As Rader's June trial date approached, a more sobering look at the case revealed that under Kansas state law in place at the time of the murders, the death penalty had been banned. It was reinstituted in 1994, and Rader's last suspected murder was 1992. Therefore, the most he could get was life without parole. With the sword of Damocles removed from his thick neck, it was to Rader's benefit to take the case to trial. He had absolutely nothing to lose. If he could convince just one juror he was innocent, he could "hang" the jury.

And then, just like that, it was all over. Claiming he was trying to spare his family any more angst—not to mention his victims and their families—Rader agreed to plead guilty on what would have been the first day of his jury trial.

Appearing in court at what was now his sentencing hearing, Rader looked like a sawed-off version of Adolph Hitler. As part of the plea deal, he had agreed to elocution during sentencing about how he carried out his crimes. Judge Waller began the sentencing proceedings by carefully reading off each of the ten murder counts and eliciting Rader's response. They went like this:

WALLER: In count number two, it is claimed that on or about the fifteenth day of January, 1974, in Sedgwick

County, Kansas, that you did then and there unlawfully kill a human being, that being Julie Otero,
maliciously, willfully, deliberately, and with premeditation by strangulation, inflicting injuries from which
the said Julie Otero did die on or about January 15,
1974.

Do you understand that you are charged with murder in the first degree, a class A felony, in count two?

RADER: Yes, your honor. Yes, sir.

The details, of course, were different for each
crime. But by the end of the beginning, Rader had
heard everything he'd been charged with and had
agreed to plead. The judge now had to be sure that
Rader knew what he was doing when he entered
his guilty pleas.

"Mr. Rader, before I can accept your plea, there
are certain things I need to find out from you and
about you," Judge Waller said. "I will do this by
asking questions of you, sir. Questions which I will
need for you to answer out loud. Should I ask you
something which you do not understand, please
ask me to explain it or repeat it. Should you need
to speak to any of your attorneys, please ask me to
let you do so and I will. All right, sir?"

"Yes, sir," Rader replied.

"Mr. Rader, as I understand it, you are sixty
years of age, having been born March 9, 1945. Is
that correct?"

"Yes, sir."

That formality dismissed, the judge asked him to

recount what happened on January 15, 1974, the beginning of his serial killing career.

"I had just done some thinking on what I was going to do to either Mrs. Otero or Josephine. I didn't have to break into the house. When they came out of the house, I came in and confronted the family and then we went from there."

"Had you planned this beforehand?"

"To some degree, yes. After I got in the house, I lost control of it. But it was, you know, in the back of my mind. I had some ideas of what I was going to do. But I just—I basically panicked that first day."

"Beforehand, did you know who was there in the house?"

"I thought Mrs. Otero and the two younger kids were in the house. I didn't realize Mr. Otero was going to be there."

"All right. How did you get into the house?"

"I cut the phone lines. Waited at the back door. Had reservations about even going in or just walking away, but pretty soon the door opened and I was in."

"Who opened it for you?"

"Joseph, one of the kids, opened the door. He probably let the dog out, because the dog was in the house at that time."

"When you went into the house, what happened then?"

"Well, I confronted the family. I pulled a pistol and pointed it at Mr. Otero and told him I wanted his car. I was hungry; I wanted food."

Rader lied. His hunger was of a different sort.

"I asked him to lie down in the living room. And at that time I realized that wouldn't be a really good idea. So I finally—the dog was a real problem, so I asked Mr. Otero, could you get the dog out? So he had one of the kids put it out."

Rader then took the family of four back to the bedroom. He took out the cord he had brought with him in his "kit" and had each member tie the other up while he watched.

"They started complaining about being tied up," Rader continued. "And I reloosened the bonds a couple of times. I tried to make Mr. Otero as comfortable as I could. Apparently, he had a cracked rib from a car accident. So I had him put a pillow down for his head."

Then the victims' pleas for their lives began.

"They talked to me about giving me the car and whatever little money they had. I realized I didn't have a mask on. They already could ID me. And I made a decision to go ahead and put them down, or strangle them."

Rader's voice was flat, like he was describing a trip to the grocery store or the mall, like nothing out of the ordinary. But the effect of that flat, self-confident voice, coupled with the obvious eloquence of the words, had a chilling effect. The judge broke the silence.

"What did you do to Joseph Otero Senior?"

"I put a plastic bag over his head and then some cords and tightened it."

"Did he, in fact, suffocate and die as a result of this?"

"Not right away. No, sir, he didn't," Rader answered matter-of-factly.

"What happened?"

"Well, after that, I did Mrs. Otero. I had never strangled anyone before, so I really don't know how much pressure you had to put on a person or how long it would take, but—"

"Was she also tied up there in the bedroom?"

"Yes, both their hands and their feet were tied up. She was on the bed."

"Where were the children?"

"Josephine was on the bed and Junior was on the floor."

"So we're talking, first of all, about Joseph Otero. So you put the bag over his head and tied it. And he did not die right away. Can you tell me what happened in regards to Joseph Junior?"

"He moved over real quick like and I think tore a hole in the bag. And I could tell that he was having some problems there. That at that time the whole family just went—they went and panicked on me. So I worked pretty quickly. I strangled Mrs. Otero and then she went out. She passed out. I thought she was dead. She passed out.

"And I strangled Josephine. She passed out. I thought she was dead. And then I went over and put the bag on Junior's head, and then, if I remember right, Mrs. Otero came back. She came back and—"

"Sir, let me ask you about Joseph Otero Senior. He had torn a hole in the bag?"

"I think I put either a cloth, or a T-shirt, or something over his head and then a bag."

"Did he subsequently die?"

"Yes. I mean I didn't just stay there and watch him. I was moving around the room," answered Rader almost indignantly.

Didn't the judge understand that killing four people at the same time was hard work, even for a man without a conscience?

"I went back and strangled her again, and finally killed her at that time."

The judge was a little confused. He wasn't the only one; everyone in the courtroom was stunned at the details. Never before had a serial killer confessed in this much detail to his crimes in open court.

"So first of all, you put the bag over Joseph Otero's head, and he tore a hole in the bag, and then you went ahead? Did you strangle Mr. Otero then?"

"*First of all*," Rader corrected, "Mr. Otero was strangled, a bag put over his head and strangled. And then I thought he was going down. Then I went over and strangled Mrs. Otero, and I thought she was down. Then I strangled Josephine, thought she was down, and then I went over to Junior and put the bag on his head.

"After that, Mrs. Otero woke back up, and you know, she was pretty upset.

" 'What's going on?' " Rader recalled her saying.

"So I came back and at that point in time I strangled her with a death strangle . . ."

"With your hands or what?"

"No, with a rope. And then I think, at that point in time, I redid Mr. Otero, put the bag over his head, went over and then—before that, she asked me to save her son, so I actually had taken the bag off, and then I was really upset at that point in time. So basically, Mr. Otero was down. Mrs. Otero was down.

"I went ahead and took Junior. I put another bag over his head and took him to the other bedroom at that time. I put the bag over his head, put a cloth over his head, a T-shirt and a bag, so he couldn't tear a hole in it. And he subsequently died from that.

"I then went back. Josephine had woken back up. I took her to the basement and hung her."

As dispassionate as a snake eating a mouse.

"Did you do anything else at that time?"

"Yes, I had some sexual fantasies. That was after she was hung."

Not like a snake.

"What did you do then?"

"I went through the house, kind of cleaned it up. It's called the right-hand rule; you go from room to room. I picked everything up. I think I took Mr. Otero's watch. I guess I took a radio. I had forgotten about that, but apparently I took a radio."

"Why did you take these things?"

"I don't know. I have no idea."

Rader knew. Like many serial killers, he liked having souvenirs of his victims. But he wouldn't say that in court.

"What happened then?"

"Got the keys to the car . . . I wanted to make sure I had a way of getting out of the house. I cleaned the house up a bit, made sure everything was packed up, and left through the front door. I went over to their car, and then drove over to Dillon's [a local restaurant] and left the car there, and then eventually walked back to my car."

In this behavior, Rader showed that he was a forensically aware serial killer, way before forensics achieved the popularity it has today as a crime fighting tool.

Rader then detailed his next murder, committed on April 4, 1974. He patiently explained to the court how he scoped out a random victim's routine.

Her name was Kathryn Bright.

*T*hirty-one years later, Kathryn Bright's brother Kevin and his wife Sharon, Kathryn's sister-in-law, had finally gotten off their Wal-Mart shift a half hour late and they were dead tired. Yet in just a few hours they would begin their weekly trip to Galveston. That was the reason they were in this poor section of the country, Sharon explained, because her son was ill with lymphoma and expected to die. He was down in Galveston, at a hospital about ninety miles away, getting treatment. They visited him every weekend.

"We'll wait for you over here," Kevin Bright said, motioning with his hand behind a concrete stanchion in the Wal-Mart parking lot.

"You like Mexican?" Sharon asked. "Kevin likes Mexican."

Having no idea where we were, I followed them down a highway; the East Texas darkness swallowed us up. Now and then, entrances to hidden subdivisions would emerge out of the forest. Then we turned up a lighted driveway and into the rear parking lot of the Mexican restaurant, up on a hill overlooking the highway. Amid the faux Mexican setting of Mayan blankets, checkered tablecloths, and overfried chips, we talked about our mutual belief in God. The Brights were Evangelical Christians.

"What do you believe in, Fred?" Sharon asked, looking at me directly.

Well, there it was; I'd been expecting it.

"I'm Jewish."

It was left unsaid that Judaism did not acknowledge Jesus as the savior. Sharon tried not to blink and wasn't successful.

"You know what, it doesn't make any difference," I explained. "I believe in God just like you do. Otherwise, I wouldn't be here."

The Brights were actually smiling after dinner, totally affable and relaxed. They invited me back to their place for coffee. It wasn't my sparkling personality, incredible good looks, religion, or anything else that got their trust. It was the food.

"No one ever bought us dinner," Kevin said simply.

"Or anything," Sharon added.

Every time Kevin had been interviewed, the Brights said, whether it was Larry King or *Time* magazine doing the interviewing, he had to pay his own expenses.

"Well, journalists are taught in journalism schools never to give anything for an interview for fear of tainting the response," I said. "But I don't see that good manners are anyone's business, do you?"

Besides, since the restaurant didn't have a liquor license, the whole check for three was about twenty-five bucks with tip. This was East Texas, not mid-town Manhattan.

I followed the Brights for about five miles down a four-lane highway that cut through the heart of town. Most of the way was pitch-black. No homes, no gas stations, no nothing. The Brights' neighborhood was all run-down single family ranches on small lots. Entering a dark kitchen, a rat terrier that had been sleeping in another room pranced in and jumped up to lick Kevin.

Inside, the furnishings were an eclectic combination of everything from cheap rented furniture to a good stereo and CD collection. Kevin went into the kitchen.

"Coffee?"

"Sure."

"Kevin loves making coffee," said Sharon.

I could hear the water boiling and Kevin preparing cups and spoons.

"A top reporter for the *Wichita Eagle* told me that Kevin had his good days and bad days."

"That's just not true!" she protested. "I don't know too many serial killer survivors who've been shot at the head working the register at Wal-Mart, do you? Now, he was just rattling off stuff to you that you were impressed with, and you are an educated man."

Kevin came over and served the coffee in tidy mugs. I took a sip.

"Hey, pretty good."

"You call that brain damaged," Sharon continued louder now, "but that's what the Wichita police and media have been saying about Kevin for years."

"You sound like a wife defending her husband. But I don't care what anybody says except Kevin," I said. "What happened Kevin?" I asked, sipping coffee. "The day Rader snuck into your apartment?"

"Sharon, my oldest sister, was cosigning a loan for me," Kevin continued, sipping his coffee. "She worked the first shift at Coleman. Kathy worked the second shift. Around noon, I picked Kathy up."

Over thirty years ago, twenty-one-year-old

big sister Kathy Bright and nineteen-year-old kid brother Kevin drove through Wichita to Valley Center to do some banking business, then back to Coleman to the house the Bright sisters shared. It was a small A-frame with two bedrooms that looked like it had been built by the second little pig; who, remember, was only a little smarter and still got eaten by the wolf.

Opening the front door of the stick-thin A-frame, Kevin and Kathy walked in. It was the middle of the day. The house was bright in parts, in others it was pools of shadow. On their left was the front bedroom, in front of them a small foyer, and then off to the right, another small bedroom and the bathroom.

"Hold it right there!"

The man came out of the shadows of the front bedroom. He was stocky, Kevin noticed, about five feet ten, wearing a thick green Army-type jacket and pointing a .22 caliber revolver in their direction. His hand held the weapon steady.

"He had been waiting for us. I'm thinking this is a cop. Maybe it's something about drugs and they're in the wrong place."

Kevin didn't know it, but Rader was in the right place, all right. He'd been stalking his sister for over a week. He knew her comings and goings, which was why her coming in with Kevin in the middle of the day was a surprise. Dennis Rader had no way of knowing Kevin Bright was just another unemployed teenager killing some time.

"What do you want?" Kevin asked.

"I'm wanted in California and I'm trying to get to New York," Rader lied. "I want your car keys, money, everything."

Rader once again with the "soft soap" before the kill.

"Here," Kevin drawled, handing him the keys and keeping his eyes peeled on the revolver pointed at his stomach.

Then, at gunpoint, Rader forced Kevin to tie up his sister in the back bedroom.

"I made sure to tie her up really loose so she could break out real easy," Kevin recalled. "Then he took me back out to the front bedroom and held the gun on me. 'Get down on the floor,' Rader ordered. He was tying up my hands with some sort of cord he had brought along."

This directly contradicted Rader's boast during his elocution that if he had brought his "kit," Kevin would be dead. Rader had lied to the judge; big surprise there. He had brought his kit, used it, and here Kevin was, alive. It must have really rankled him.

"Then I heard him go in the other room and do something and rummage around and then he was back. I was still on the floor, I'd been struggling to get free, and then he put this cord around my neck and started strangling me."

Kevin spoke in a slow methodical voice; getting something off his chest, I would learn, for the first time in his life.

"I found out later that it was a knotted nylon stocking. He wrapped it around my neck and began strangling me," Kevin continued, "and I was struggling and broke loose. He was as far away from me as I am from you," he continued, rising and moving over to where I was sitting in a stiff-backed Salvation Army chair.

Kevin looked down at me with an intense, controlled gaze. It was easy to imagine him looking at Rader's gun without flinching. There was something about the guy that said, "Don't mess with me." I've only seen it a few times in my life. The last was a guy who was in the mob.

"I jumped up. He'd had the gun in his waistband while he had been tying me. He reached into it and pulled out his .22 revolver. He later said in court during his plea that he also had a .357 Magnum in a shoulder holster and that was really the gun we fought for. He's lying. There was no Magnum. The only gun we fought over was the .22.

"We fought for it. It was a life or death struggle. I got my hand on it and turned his gun hand around into his stomach."

Sitting back down, Kevin sipped his coffee, looking out thoughtfully into the living room's drab brown rented carpet that was like his crystal ball. He was seeing it again.

"I got my finger on the trigger. I tried to fire but it just wouldn't go."

"Rader said in court that he got his finger in the trigger guard and that prevented you from firing."

"That's not true," Kevin answered. "He had on black gloves. His finger couldn't have gotten through."

What had probably happened was Kevin failed to flick off the safety, which was why Rader, military-trained in hand-to-hand combat and a small-arms specialist, managed to finally take control of the gun. He brought it up, flicked off the safety and fired.

The .22 revolver is a small compact weapon with a storied history back into the nineteenth century. Extremely effective on a human target at close quarters, the same type of weapon Rader wielded was used by Sirhan Sirhan only a few years earlier to kill Bobby Kennedy with one shot to the back and one to the head from a few inches away. Kevin's situation was different.

"The first bullet just grazed me on the side here," he said, pointing to a long, slightly whitish scar in the skin. "The second went in over here."

Kevin raised the prematurely white hair on the right side of his face up over his ear, pointing to a clear indentation in his skull where the .22 caliber bullet entered his skull and then his brain.

"I was conscious the whole time."

Kevin sipped his coffee thoughtfully.

"I decided to play dead. He leaves me and goes back in the bedroom. The last thing I ever heard my sister say was what she said to him. 'What did you do to my brother?' Rader answered, 'He got shot, he's all right, and I'll call an ambulance.' "

Even as she faced death, Kathy Bright was more concerned about her brother and the struggles she had been hearing in the front bedroom. Then came the two gunshots, and she must have figured Kevin was dead.

"After a while he came back in to check me. He kicked me. I guess I must have groaned and that told him I was still alive. He put that nylon thing around my neck again and was strangling me. I was struggling when he shot me in my mouth," and Kevin pointed to a spot on the right side of his face just above his right lip, next to his nose.

Rader watched as Kevin collapsed to the ground. Between the three bullets he had pumped into his surprised victim, strangling him twice, with all that blood, he must have thought, My God, the guy had to be dead! But he wasn't; far from it. Kevin was still alive and, amazingly, still conscious. He heard Rader's footsteps retreating into the back bedroom where he figured Kathy was still tied up.

"I looked up and around the room, surveying it for an object, anything I could use, like a bottle maybe or a lamp, something like that, I could use to clobber him with. Anything."

But there was nothing.

"I couldn't see anything that could help me. I figured that the best thing I could do was to get out and get help. I got up somehow, and saw that the bedroom door was open. Stepping to the right a few feet to the door, I saw that it was closed, with the safety chain latched in place."

Kevin pulled the chain, never turning to look back. In so doing, he picked up precious seconds to affect his escape.

"I went out on the street. There were two guys on the corner. I ran up and told them what had happened. One guy took me to the hospital and the other went to call the cops. The cops looked but they couldn't find anybody. Whoever had done it had got away. After that, I was three days in intensive care and 215 more days in the hospital, 218 days total.

"It was while I was in the hospital that I started thinking, 'Is he gonna come and get me? What would I do if I saw this guy? What would I do?' "

While Kevin was recuperating, Rader had a compulsion to communicate. He wanted to show everyone how powerful he was, how much he knew, and to taunt the police. In October 1974 the *Wichita Eagle-Beacon* got a letter from someone taking responsibility for the Otero family homicides. Included were details known only to the cops and the killer. It was genuine.

One of the defining qualities of a serial killer is the cooling off period between murders. It is during this time that the killer's inner rages build once again to the point of murder. It can take as little as a few days or as much as a few years. Rader took his time and didn't strike until two and a half years later, on March 17, 1977, in Cedric County, Kansas.

"Shirley Vian was completely random. There

was actually someone across from Dillon's who was a potential target. It was called Project Green, I think. I had project numbers assigned to it.

"That particular day," Rader continued in his elocution to the court, "I drove to Dillon's and parked in the parking lot and watched this particular residence and then got out of the car and walked over to it."

No one was home. Rader had been looking forward to a good murder. He was all keyed up. He did what any respectable serial killer would do. "I just started going through the neighborhood.

"I had been there before. I'd been through the back alleys and knew where certain people lived. While I was walking down Hyacinth, I met a young boy and asked him if he could ID some pictures. Kind of a ruse, I guess," Rader stated modestly. "I had to feel it out and see where he went."

Rader followed the boy, "and we went from there."

"Now you call these projects," Judge Waller reminded the killer. "Were these sexual fantasies also?"

"In my world, I called them potential hits. Or projects."

The judge wasn't interested in the terminology so much as the motive. Rader had cleverly not answered the "$1,000,000 question."

"Why did you do these potential hits? Was this to gratify some sexual interest or—"

"Yes, sir," Rader interrupted proudly. "I had a lot of them. If one didn't work out, I just moved to another one."

Whether Rader was talking about potential hits, sexual fantasies, or both, was unclear.

"What happened next?"

"I watched and went to the house where the boy had gone in, knocked on the door. I told them I was a private detective. I just showed them the picture I'd shown the boy."

In the second it took Shirley Vian to figure out what to do, Rader pulled his gun "and I just kind of forced myself in. I just walked in, just opened the door and walked in and then pulled a pistol."

This time, Rader had only one gun. It was the one that could do the most damage. When Rader shot Kevin Bright, it was with the .22 revolver. A .22 slug does not produce a big wound.

"But being as this is a .44 Magnum, the most powerful handgun in the world, and would blow your head clean off," as Clint Eastwood's *Dirty Harry* had said, Vian offered no resistance. Perhaps it was the fact that he felt in total control that led Rader to opened up a little bit.

"I told Mrs. Vian that I had a problem with sexual fantasies and I was going to tie her up and that I might have to tie the kids up." Rader asked her to "cooperate with me. She was extremely nervous. I think she even smoked a cigarette. And we went back to one of the back areas of the porch.

"I explained that I had done this before. And I think she—at that point in time, I think she was sick, because she had her night robe on. I think if I remember right, she had been sick. I think she came out of the bedroom when I went in the house.

"So anyway, we went back to her bedroom. And I proceeded to tie the kids up and they started crying and got real upset, so I said, 'Oh, this is not going to work.' So we moved them to the bathroom. She helped me. And then I tied the door shut. We put toys and blankets and odds and ends in there for the kids, to make them as comfortable as we could. We tied one of the bathroom doors shut so they couldn't open it, and she helped me shove a bed up against the other bathroom door."

But it had all been too much for Vian.

"She got sick and threw up. I got her a glass of water, comforted her a little bit, and then I went ahead and tied her up. I tied her legs to the bed post and worked up with the rope all the way up. And then what I had left over, I looped over her neck. Then I put a plastic bag over her head and strangled her."

Why had Vian patiently smoked a cigarette and then submitted willingly to Rader's execution like a concentration camp victim being led into a gas chamber? From Rader's description—and that's all there is to go on—it sounds like Vian thought if she resisted, which she saw as futile, her kids would be killed. The problem, really, and the reason why Vian did not survive, was that she was not ready to kill her attacker, let alone resist. At any point, as Rader marched her throughout the house when he did have her covered with the revolver, she could have resisted him, picked up a glass bowl, for example, and smashed it into Rader's face. Even if she were shot, she would have done some damage.

"What happened then?" the judge continued.

"Well, the kids were really banging on the door, hollering, screaming. And then the telephone rang. And they had talked about earlier that the neighbors were going to check on them, so I cleaned everything up real quick-like. Whatever I had laying around, ropes, tape, cords, I threw into a briefcase. You know, whatever I had, that I had brought in the house."

"Now, when you say you cleaned everything up . . . was this a kit that you had prepared?"

"Yes. I call it my 'hit kit.' "

Hit kit under his arm, Rader walked to his car and drove home like nothing had happened. Whether he opened the door to his house that night and yelled, "Honey, I'm home, what's for dinner?" is debatable. But considering his lifestyle as the "Brady dad," it is not an unlikely scenario. Were Robert Reed alive, he would be perfect for the dichotomous part of the family man serial killer.

It would not be until January 31, 1978, that a poem referring to the Vian killing was sent to the *Wichita Eagle-Beacon*. Ten days later, on February 10, 1978, a letter from BTK was sent to KAKA-TV. In it, BTK claimed the deaths of Vian, Nancy Fox, and an unnamed victim as his own. Police Chief Richard Amnion declared to the public that a serial killer was at large.

"*I* kept wondering what I would do if I walked down the street and saw him coming toward me," Kevin Bright recalled. "What would I do? And I also thought, 'Surely he knows where I live.' It's not just about locking doors."

By December 1977, Kevin Bright was consistently worried BTK would return to finish the job. Physically, he had mostly recovered from the serial killer's attempt to kill him. He could walk, talk, think, do anything as well as or better than anyone else. But he'd been left with a dual reminder of the damage the bullets did.

"Two things, really. Can't tolerate heat and humidity. I've got nerve damage in my brain from the bullet that makes it difficult for my body to regulate my temperature. I don't sweat normally. My internal temperature gets real hot and I get weak," said Kevin, putting his feet up on an old trunk doubling for a coffee table, piled high with magazines and papers.

"The second is, he can't eat food at work because he'll have to go," Sharon interrupted. "One thing I'm very proud of my husband, there's so many people in this state on disability and everything else. He's been disabled, and still puts in a full day of work.

"When I met him, Kevin was on a tennis court and his hair was not white, but I thought, 'Why is this man wearing a toupee?' Half of his hair was one way, and the other, where he was shot, was another. I found out what happened and it broke my heart."

Sharon had a wanderlust that seemed to match Kevin's, but there was something else there with Kevin. Exactly what it was wouldn't become clear for decades, over which patterns of life, and parallel ones of crime, built up. Meanwhile there were bags to pack. Both also had things to do.

Around the same time, on December 8, 1977, Rader murdered Nancy Fox, admitting later in court that she had been another one of his "projects." He later testified to what can only be described as a how-to course in serial killing.

"First, she was spotted. I did a little homework," Rader later told the judge. "I dropped by once to check her mailbox, to see what her name was. Found out where she worked, at Halberd's, stopped by there once to size her up. The more I knew about a person, the more I felt comfortable. So I did that a couple of times. Then I just selected a night, which was this particular night, to try it, and it worked out."

Following his M.O., after bypassing the home's security, cutting the phone lines, and breaking in, he waited for Fox. When she came home, "I confronted her, told her I had a sexual problem, that I would have to tie her up and have sex with her.

She was a little upset and we talked awhile and she smoked a cigarette. While she smoked, I went through her purse, identifying some stuff.

" 'Well, let's get this over with so I can call the police,' she finally said. I told her 'Okay.' And she asked, 'Can I go to the bathroom?' I said 'Yes.' "

Inside Fox's bathroom was the means to save her life if she chose it—the bathroom mirror. Broken, it could easily be used to slash his throat. "When she came out, I handcuffed her, had her lay on the bed, and I tied her feet. I was also undressed to a certain degree and then I got on top of her and I reached over and tied her feet. Anyway, I took [my] belt and strangled her at that time."

Rader enjoyed the struggle of his victims and how he would eventually overpower them.

"After I strangled her with the belt, I took the belt off and retied that with panty hose, real tight, removed the handcuffs and tied those with pantyhose. I can't remember the colors right now. I think I may have retied her feet. They were probably already tied, her feet were. And then at that time, I masturbated."

Rader took some personal items as souvenirs of the murder, cleaned up any evidence he might have left, and went to his car, which he had parked several blocks away. Then he called 911 from a pay phone to inform police about what he had done. He was rubbing their face in it, but it pales next to what Rader did next.

Perhaps it explains why he eluded capture for so long—he never did what was expected. He constantly broke serial killer archetypes and defied even the most cutting edge research by so-called profilers when he chose Marine Hedge as his next victim. A major theory in criminal profiling says that serial killers usually have a safe zone, a haven around which they will not commit a crime out of fear of drawing attention to themselves.

This safe zone extends, minimally, a few blocks from the killer's place of residence. Rader, though, did not give a damn about serial killer archetypes developed by the FBI, private profilers, or anybody else. He decided to kill within his safe zone. And he waited a full seven years since his last known murder to do it.

On April 27, 1985, Marine Hedge became BTK victim number eight. She lived just a few houses down the street from the one Rader occupied with his wife Paula and the kids. He looked forward to this hit being an easy one because he could track Hedge's movements by literally looking out his window. Since they were neighbors, Rader even spoke to her on occasion.

Evincing the same M.O., Rader used his security training to break in undetected to Hedge's house. As had become common for him now, he cased the place and picked a spot to wait for his victim. He had time, lots of it. When she finally came through the door, she was accompanied by a man. Rader kept himself hidden until the man left and the woman was asleep.

"I waited until the wee hours of the morning

and then proceeded to sneak into her bedroom and flip the lights on real quick-like, I think the bathroom lights. She screamed. I jumped on the bed and strangled her manually.

"After that, since I was still in the sexual fantasy, I went ahead and stripped her. I am not sure if I tied her up at that point in time, but she was nude. I put her on a blanket, went through her purse and personal items in the house. I figured out how I was going to get her out of there."

Reaching new heights of blasphemy, "I moved her to the trunk of the car and took the car over to Christ Lutheran Church, this was the older church, and took some pictures of her in different forms of bondage. That is what probably got me in trouble is the bondage thing. But anyway, then I moved her back out to her car."

Cops hate body dump jobs, where a victim is dumped someplace far away from where she had actually been murdered. Frequently, the bodies have been stripped of identification; that, plus a dearth of forensic evidence, since the scene of the crime is actually miles away, can make this sort of case difficult to solve even for the smartest detective.

Rader dumped Hedge's body in a ditch someplace near 53rd Street between Webb and Greenwich. He used some trees and brush to cover the body and, hopefully, conceal it for nature to go to work and remove any vestigial traces of the crime on the corpse. Next, it was time to taunt the cops again and show 'em up.

On September 16, 1986, Vicki Wegerle was Dennis Rader's new project. This time he planned things out more carefully than ever before.

"My plan was to tell her I was a telephone repair man to get into the house. I changed into my 'hit clothes.'"

"What are 'hit clothes'?" Judge Waller interrupted.

"Basically things I would need to get rid of later. Not the same kind of clothes I had on. I don't know what better word to use; crime clothes. I just call them hit clothes. I walked from my car as a telephone repairman. As I walked there, I donned a telephone helmet. I had a briefcase.

"Then, I went to one other address just to kind of size up the house. I had walked by it a couple of times, but I wanted to size it up more. As I approached it, I could hear a piano sound and I went to this other door and knocked on it and told them that we were recently working on telephone repairs in the area. Then, I went to hers [Wegerle's], knocked on the door, asked her if I could come check her telephone lines inside."

After Wegerle let him in, "I found out where the telephone was and simulated that I was checking the telephone. I had a make-believe instrument. And after she was looking away, I drew a pistol on her."

One thing in common with all his "hits" was Rader's cowardly behavior. He got a kick out of surprising his victims; they never had a chance. Rader enjoyed the power he held over Wegerle. He told her to go back to the bedroom, where he was going to tie her up. She complied, but something went wrong with the tying-up part. The Boy Scout leader was lousy at knots. They came loose and Wegerle decided to fight him.

Adrenaline pumping to the max, feeling more powerful and omnipotent than ever, Dennis Rader grabbed one of her stockings and wound it around her neck and pulled. Hard. Harder. It took a few minutes, but eventually she stopped moving. When he thought she was dead, Rader rearranged her clothes and took several photos of her.

"There was a lot of commotion. She had mentioned something about her husband coming home, so I got out of there pretty quick. The dogs were raising a lot of Cain in the back, the doors and windows were all open in the house, and there had been a lot of noise when we were fighting. So I left pretty quickly after that, put everything in the briefcase, and I had already gone through her purse and got the keys to the car and used it."

Vicki Wegerle was fatally injured from the strangling but was not yet dead when Rader left her home. That would come later in the hospital. But what also made this homicide different was that police did not link it to BTK. Something about this crime did not, to police eyes, resemble the M.O. of the previous crimes.

*   *   *

*B*y 1991, Kevin Bright had become a modern Larry Darrell. But whereas the World War I hero of the Maugham novel *The Razor's Edge* goes to India to find the reason he was spared and his friends were not, Kevin has been roaming the southwestern United States with his wife and constant companion Sharon looking for the answers to those same questions.

"We lived in Oklahoma, Arkansas, Oklahoma, Colorado, Arkansas, Colorado, Oklahoma, Wisconsin, and now Texas," Sharon recited, in order of when they lived in those places.

She showed me a news article from a Colorado paper about a bed and breakfast they ran in the Rockies during the 1980s. The couple's picture was in the piece.

"Kevin had dark hair back then," she said, looking at the old photograph, and then smiling up at her husband. "Kevin is unsettled," she continued. "We moved around a lot and had a lot of fun. We're workers. We don't owe anybody anything."

The man responsible for their wanderings, BTK struck next on January 19, 1991, when Dennis Rader chose a very noisy way to get into the house of Dolores Davis. He threw a concrete block through her plate-glass window. She came out of the bedroom and thought a car had hit her house.

"I used the ruse again that I was wanted and on the run. I told her I needed food, car, and warmth. I handcuffed her, I told her I would like to get some food, the keys to her car, talked with her a little bit, calmed her down a little bit, and eventually I checked out where the car was, simulated getting some food, odds and ends in the house like I was leaving, went back, removed her handcuffs, then tied her up, and then eventually strangled her."

Again, he took some personal items from the victim's bedroom. Then he put her in a blanket and dragged her to the trunk of her car and hoisted her in. This time Rader's own social commitments rushed his actions. He left one of his guns in her house. With the body still in the trunk, he drove back to her house, collected his gun, and walked back out to his car. He then drove off and dumped Davis's body under a bridge.

For the next thirteen years BTK remained quiet, so quiet that many in Wichita thought he had died. After all, the crimes had started in the middle of 1976. For all anyone knew, BTK might have been a fifty-year-old man when he started.

On March 10, 2004, a letter arrived at the *Wichita Eagle*. It contained pictures of Vicki Wegerle's body that only the killer would have access to, and a copy of her driver's license. The meaning was instantly clear: BTK's ego had been found wanting. He hadn't killed in a while. He needed satiation. He got it by claiming an old victim.

"I'm baaacckkkkk . . ."

Another year went by. The case once again stalled. No new leads developed. On February 26,

2005, BTK began sending a stream of letters to the cops directly. It was like he was asking to be caught. It was only a matter of time until they were traced. The cops finally backtracked them to their source, a computer at Wichita's Christ Church Lutheran where Dennis Rader had created and printed them. Rader was then arrested and charged with the BTK killings.

Dennis Rader's wife and kids had no idea about his other life as BTK. When the story broke, they were more stunned than anyone else. But Rader was never really a family man. He was a sociopath; he was just pretending.

Police recovered numerous pictures at Rader's house, pictures he had taken of himself, using a camera timing mechanism. Some of the shots—in which he posed in Mardi Gras masks, wigs, and one victim's undergarments—were dated 1990, others 1994. Many were taken in the basement of his parents' home.

In the shots, Rader poses in various bondage outfits. He is tied to a chair, hanging from a ceiling, even half buried in a makeshift grave. Bondage seemed to be Rader's milieu. He said as much during his statement to forensic investigators, later broadcast on network TV.

"I don't think it was actually the person that I was after, I think it was the dream. I know that's not really nice to say about a person, but they were basically an object. They were just an object. That's all they were. I had more satisfaction building up to it and afterward than I did the actual killing of the person.

"You have to have the *control,* which is the bonding. That's been a big thing with me. My sexual fantasy is, if I'm going to kill a victim or do something to the victim, is having them *bound and tied.* In my dreams, I had what they called torture chambers. And to relieve your sexual fantasies, you have to go for the kill."

Dennis Rader never saw his victims as human beings, but as objects to be brutalized and exploited.

"All of these incidents, these ten counts," Judge Waller said to Rader, "occurred because you wanted to satisfy *sexual fantasies.* Is that correct?"

"Yes," Rader answered.

In sentencing him, Waller then considered the letters that had been sent to him by relatives of the victims. Sharon Bright's was the only one from a survivor's wife.

"Writing my letter to the judge about how Kevin's being shot affected him got me to thinking about why," said Sharon angrily. "It was like Kevin expected him [Rader] to come back even though he let him live. He didn't let him live. Kevin fought for his life and won."

That's what it was about for Kevin; for Rader it was a whole different matter. The one thing that nagged at him, clearly by what he had said in his own words during his elocution, was the one that got away. About Kevin Bright, he had told the court:

"If I had brought my hit kit and used it, Kevin would probably be dead today. I'm not bragging on that. It's just a matter of fact."

Judge Waller then made it a matter of *law* that Dennis Rader be sentenced to life in prison. It was the maximum Kansas law allowed.

"What's funny," Sharon said, "is that we heard him twice say Kevin was a really big guy. Kevin was a little scrawny nineteen-year-old kid."

"You know why he said it, don't you?" I asked.

"Because it made it look like only a big guy could wrestle him."

I nodded.

"Before we came down here, we were in Wisconsin," Kevin said, his coffee cup almost finished. "I was studying to be a pastor at PBI, a three-year Bible study school."

Kevin had already put in one year of the three-year course work. Those studies ended when Sharon was summoned to Galveston to be near her son, Kevin's stepson.

"Did what happened to you make you want to be a preacher?" I asked.

"Looking back, you can see how God's hand is in there. I thought, hey, protected," Kevin answered.

"He protected you?"

"Yeah. 'Why am I alive? Why didn't I die?' There's some purpose. You think to yourself, 'I'm not a bad person, why me?' " Kevin answered.

To Kevin Bright, the answer can be found in his religious belief.

"We were deaf. God sends people in your path. Once, we lived across the street from a choir director. This person's really involved in the church. He never invited us to church and we lived right across the street. We kinda wanted to go to a church," Kevin said.

"Do you hope you can go back to Bible study school when things are better?"

"Whatever he wants," Sharon answered. "I'm following his lead."

"Timewise, we believe there's not much time left," Kevin drawled. "Time is running out. Why spend another two years getting prepared to do something you already can do?"

Sharon had been sitting on a bridge chair. She had long since exchanged the shoes with Christmas bells for furry blue slippers.

"Something you have to understand about Kevin, his family," Sharon interrupted. "They don't talk about anything. They've buried Kathy, and even when we went back this summer, Kevin's brother and sister won't even talk to him about it. They won't even talk to him about going to Wisconsin. Kathy was buried thirty-one years ago. You never bring her name up again."

"Why?" I asked.

"That's the way their family is. Kevin is very quiet and humble; he doesn't talk about things. He has had this locked inside of him for thirty-one years. The most heartbreaking thing for me was when Kevin went back to Wichita to give his victim's impact statement for Rader's trial.

"His dad and his brother were there in the courtroom, and neither one of them got up and stood next to him or behind him. I couldn't be in the room with him and I was so mad at the judge. I wanted to kill him for not giving me a seat in the courtroom to support my husband.

"Now, his dad has never spoken to anybody, he will never speak to anybody, his sister won't speak to him," Sharon continued.

"But there's got to be something else going on there," I prodded.

"We've always felt like maybe they thought he should have been able to save her, you know, there was no way!"

It was hard to imagine anyone rejecting a relative for being a survivor of something so horrendous. Gently, Kevin stroked his dog's head.

"That's Kevin's child," said Sharon warmly. "We've had him for twelve years."

Rader had made a fatal mistake. He unknowingly left alive the one witness that would have positively identified him had the case ever gone to trial. Kevin Bright, all five-six and 140 pounds soaking wet, was the one man BTK was truly afraid of and would never approach again. Rader knew that Bright had a punch like Roberto Duran's. With a weapon, Kevin Bright would kill him.

"Looking back, God's hand was in everything,"

said Kevin. "He protected me that afternoon. I'm not a bad person. My sister wasn't one either. There's got to be more to life than existing. We were deaf. God sends people in your path."

The rat terrier clung to Kevin's heels as he and Sharon saw me out to the driveway. It was December in East Texas, and damn cold. I shivered and I wondered. After being shot, strangled, and everything else, what gave Kevin the strength to rise up off the floor of his sister's apartment? With Kathy dying or dead in the next bedroom, how did he find the will to burst his bonds and begin a successful struggle for his life? To Kevin, the answer is "God's hand."

"Kathy was only twenty-one. She had her whole life ahead of her. She had plans," Kevin said to me at the door.

"So do you, Kevin."

In the rearview mirror, Kevin and Sharon waved goodbye. Kevin had survived but paid a heavy price. The emotional upheaval from being the only survivor was etched in his skin, in the tautness of his body, his direct gaze, never missing anything, seeing everything, always on alert. His was a hard celebrity to escape notoriety. Sooner or later another reporter would show up with more questions. Maybe it would be during an appeal by Rader or some other legal action. Or maybe for the next segment of *Serial Killer's Round Table*.

It was a cold night, the defrosters winking against the East Texas chill and fog. Driving south through scrubland and then suburbs, Houston suddenly sprawled out across an eight-lane highway that cut right through the heart of the city.

Eisenhower would have been proud. I got on a plane and headed out of town.

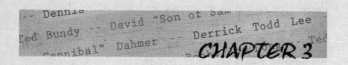
Survivor: Lisa McVey
Serial Killer: Bobby Joe Long
aka "Classified Ad Rapist"

*I*t felt strange to be on the people mover. I wasn't in Disneyland but I might as well have been.

Back in 1967 there was no Disney World or EuroDisney, only Disneyland in Anaheim. Walt Disney used his TV show, *The Wonderful World of Disney,* "Sunday nights at 7:00 P.M., six central time on NBC," to shill for his one of a kind amusement park. When Walt and his Imagineers were imagining a new Tomorrowland attraction, all scrupulously documented by Disney's cameramen for future episodes, Walt kept referring to the attraction as the "people mover." According to Imagineer Bob Gurr, "the name got stuck."

The people mover is an automated grade, separated trail transit system that travels over short distances. Disney used it in Tomorrowland to shuttle people around, sometimes through the interior of rides. His idea was so popular that in 1971, Tampa International Airport became the first airport in the world to install a people mover.

Exiting my plane, I found myself at one of four Airside satellites where airliner embarkment and disembarkment occur. Less than a few hundred feet away was the people mover pickup station. An automated voice advised that a train was coming, there was a sharp whoosh of air, and a bullet train appeared behind the glass-enclosed platform.

Stepping into a hermetically sealed compartment, the fully automated people mover (APM) started up and popped out into the late afternoon sun, whooshing across the airport tarmac, heading toward the Landside Terminal. In a few moments the APM stopped and the doors opened into what sounded like a loud shopping mall. It was actually where all the airport's baggage and ticketing functions took place, not to mention rental cars and other transportation options. There were also all kinds of stores selling all kinds of products, from expensive leather jackets to $9.95 sunglasses.

Like most people, serial killers prefer working where it's warm rather than cold. For them, it's easier to locate and pick up victims when weather is not a factor. Since the idea of the APM system was to limit the walking distance between the automobile and airliner to seven hundred feet, Ted Bundy, Bobby Joe Long, Andrew Cunanen, and who knows how many other serial killers who used the Tampa APM facilities surely appreciated its ease of operation and effortless transport between their destinations.

But as interesting as the airport's transportation system was, the roadway outside, Interstate 275, was just as boring. It was a "feeder" into Interstate 75, the major north-south road in Hillsborough County, the diverse area surrounding the city of Tampa. The county has its own police force, the Hillsborough County Sheriff's Office, which has one of the best homicide bureaus in the country.

Before walking into the Hillsborough County Courthouse in downtown Tampa, Lisa McVey looked up Kennedy Boulevard. On the horizon, her intense green eyes picked out Interstate 75 snaking north. It beckoned any serial killer who drove a car, bought a bus ticket, or simply thumbed a ride south to sunny Florida.

Bobby Joe Long had traveled it many times.

Born in West Virginia in 1953, Long's parents divorced when he was two. While his dad stayed in West Virginia, Long moved with his mom down the interstate to Florida. Much of his time growing up was split between those two states. In 1983, when he was twenty-nine, Long traveled down the interstate for the last time to Tampa, where he got himself a nice apartment. Once he was comfortable, he began looking through the classified ads to meet women.

His first victim was a woman who'd placed an ad to sell her house; Long responded. Once inside the victim's home, Long pulled out a revolver, forced the victim into her bedroom, and raped her. Long used this M.O. to rape fifty women over the course of the next year. The newspapers dubbed the unknown assailant, the "Classified Ad Rapist."

In May 1984 a new danger to the women of the Tampa area began to take shape. And as the headlines grew about that "bad guy," the Classified Ad Rapist faded into the background.

May 13, 1984
Mother's Day

Late in the afternoon, the first—the nude, bound body of a young Asian woman—was discovered by two young boys in a remote area of southern Hillsborough County. Corporal Lee "Pops" Baker of the Hillsborough County Sheriff's Office was the senior homicide detective assigned to the case.

Baker found the victim lying facedown with her hands tied behind her back with what looked like rope and fabric. There was a rope around her neck. It had a "leashlike" extension approximately fourteen inches long. There were also ropes, probably used as some sort of restraints, around the wrists and neck.

Under the victim's face was a piece of fabric, which had probably been used as a gag. Her feet were spread apart over five feet; it appeared as if the body had been deliberately "displayed" in this manner. On the basis of how long the body had cooled, the medical examiner figured her to be dead for approximately forty-eight to seventy-two hours.

During the autopsy, a large open wound was discovered on the victim's face. Decomposition—or "decomp," as it is called in the trade—was extensive in this area. Cause of death was determined to be strangulation. The knots in the ropes were examined and identified as extremely common and not unique to any particular profession or occupation. The tire casts of the tire tread impressions were also examined and photographs of these impressions were kept for future reference.

The fibers that were removed from the items were also examined. Eventually it would prove to be the most critical evidence of the entire case. Since the victim's body was found in a remote area, she had probably been transported in a vehicle, and the carpeting of this vehicle was probably the last item she had been in contact with.

Baker identified the victim as Ngeun Thi Long, a twenty-year-old Laotian exotic dancer at a lounge in Tampa. A drug user, she had been missing for approximately three days when her body was discovered. Because of the decomp, it was impossible to tell if she had been raped.

Two weeks later, on May 27, 1984, at approximately 11:30 A.M., the body of a young white female was discovered in an isolated area of eastern Hillsborough County. She was nude, clothing lying wanly nearby. She was on her back, hands bound to her sides with a clothesline type of rope. She had what appeared to be a green men's T-shirt binding her upper arms. Baker saw that her throat had been cut. Her head had sustained what the M.E. would later describe as "multiple blows."

The ligature at the neck was made of the same type of rope as the first homicide, and was tied in a type of hangman's noose. There was a three- to four-foot length of rope extending from the noose. This also seemed consistent with the first homicide. She'd been dead about eight to ten hours.

Pops Baker knew it was the same guy. But again, there was no ID on the victim, no way to identify her, except the old-fashioned way. Police sketch artists made a composite drawing of the victim. Vilma Bean, the crackerjack public relations officer for the department, quickly released it to the media. Out in California, someone recognized her.

Her name was Michele Denise Simms. A twenty-two-year-old California native, she had last been seen the previous night talking with two white males near Kennedy Boulevard, in an area popular with working girls. Simms had a record as a prostitute. Since this had been a "fresh" site, the chances of recovering significant evidence would be tremendously improved.

Not having had a chance to degrade through time, the tire casts were closely examined.

One of the impressions from the right rear area

was identified as being from a Goodyear Viva tire, with the white wall facing inward. The tire impression from the left rear area was eventually identified by a tire expert in Akron, Ohio, as being made by Vogue tire, an expensive tire only on Cadillacs.

Fiber analysis revealed red lustrous trilobal nylon fibers, which matched the fibers found with the first victim. In addition, a second type of fiber, a red trilobal delustered fiber, was found, indicating that the killer was driving a vehicle containing *two* different types of carpet fibers.

Simms's body had not been exposed to the elements. Tests done on semen stains found on Michele Simms's clothing revealed the B and H blood group substances. Brown, medium-length Caucasian head hairs were on the body that did not match Simms's. Baker logically figured the hairs came from the killer.

On June 24, 1984, the body of another young white female was found, the third victim in this series of homicides, although this would not be known for a few months. The problem was "linkage"—the ability to link specific homicides in a decipherable pattern.

This time, the female victim was found in an orange grove in southeastern Hillsborough County, fully clothed. The body was in such an advanced stage of decomposition, its total weight, soaking wet, including clothes, was only twenty-five pounds. There were no ligatures present, and the victim was not found near an interstate, as the first two victims had been.

Police eventually identified the victim as Elizabeth B. Loudenback, a twenty-two-year-old Tampa assembly line worker. She was last seen at approximately 7:00 P.M. on June 8, 1984. On the basis of her decomposition, it was a safe assumption she had been dead about sixteen days. Hair and fiber evidence were gathered at the scene by the "techies," but not the ones who had worked the previous crime scenes. They did note however, that two types of red nylon carpet fibers were recovered from Loudenback's body.

Unfortunately, since it was a different group of "techies," no request was made to the FBI to compare the evidence from the previous two homicides until much later in the case. If this examination had been done initially, linkage would have taken place and a determination made that Loudenback was the serial killer's third victim.

On October 7, 1984, the nude body of a young black woman was discovered in a remote section of Hillsborough County. Her head was in an advanced state of decomposition, much more so than the remainder of the body. Could she have been shot? Sure enough, the autopsy revealed a gunshot wound to the neck. There was also a puncture wound to the back of the neck. Except for her bra, her clothing was found next to the body. The bra was found hanging rather symbolically from the entrance gate, tied in a knot.

The victim was identified as eighteen-year-old prostitute Chanel Devon Williams. Chanel had disappeared while walking back to her motel room. Baker sent the evidence from the Williams case to the FBI Laboratory a *second* time. It was the charm. Both types of the red nylon carpet fibers seen in the first two homicides were found on various articles of Chanel's clothing. A brown Caucasian pubic hair also matched.

Two weeks later, on the morning of October 14, 1984, the serial killer struck again. The body of a white prostitute, later identified as Karen Beth Dinsfriend, a twenty-eight-year-old cocaine user, was found, nude from the waist down. She was discovered in an orange grove in northeastern Hillsborough County. She had been dragged back approximately thirty feet from dirt road and placed nude on a gold-colored bedspread.

Baker noted that the victim's hands were bound in front with a red and white handkerchief. Her right wrist and legs were bound with another white string. Her feet were bound with a drawstring; there were ligature marks on her throat. The ligatures were a "signature" of the offender. It looked like someone had struck a sharp blow to her forehead.

Red carpet fibers were found when the body was examined at the medical examiner's office. They were microscopically compared to the previous carpet fibers. It was a direct match. That brought the serial killer's kill total up to five. Sixteen days later, number six turned up.

On October 30, 1984, the nude, mummified body of a white female was discovered near Highway 301 in northern Hillsborough County just south of the Pasco County line. The M.O., though, was different. No clothing, ligatures, or any other type of physical evidence were found at the scene. That didn't mean it wasn't the same guy. Some serial killers changed their M.O. as they went along; others kept it the same.

But something must have been happening in the serial killer's psyche. His "cooling off" period between crimes was speeding up. Just one week later, on November 6, 1984, the remains of a female were discovered near Morris Bridge Road in Pasco County just north of the Hillsborough County line. "Remains" is perhaps a misleading word; "bones" is more like it.

The victim's bones were scattered over a large area. Ligature marks were found on her arm bones. A shirt, a pair of panties, and some jewelry were also found. While reading the police teletype, Pops Baker learned of this grisly discovery. Because of the ligatures, Baker believed that this case was related to his homicides. They eventually identified the victim as eighteen-year-old Virginia Lee Johnson, a white girl originally from Connecticut.

Johnson worked as a prostitute in the North Nebraska Avenue area in Hillsborough County. In the victim's head hair a single red, lustrous carpet fiber was found, relating this case to the others.

On November 24, 1984, the nude body of a

young white female was found on an incline off
North Orient Road in the city of Tampa, involving
yet a third jurisdiction in the homicides. The Tampa
M.E. assigned to the case checked the victim's temperature and determined she had been dead less
than twenty-four hours. It was a fresh kill.

Faint tire impressions were observed in the grass
next to the roadway. The killer had probably pulled
off the road and thrown the body over the edge and
onto the incline. That's why she was discovered
facedown. All she wore were knee-high nylons. A
wadded pair of blue jeans and a blue flowered top
was found near the body. It was as if someone had
thrown them away as an afterthought.

When the Tampa cops turned the victim, the
first thing they noticed was the pronounced ligature mark on the front portion of the neck. She'd
been strangled. There were also ligature marks on
both wrists and on both arms. It looked like the
Hillsborough County Sheriff's Office serial killer.
The Tampa PD immediately called the HCSO.

The victim was identified as Kim Marie Swann,
a twenty-one-year-old "narcotics user, who worked
as a nude dancer." That's cop slang for a drug addict who whored her body for men in sleazy strip
clubs. She was last seen walking out of a convenience store near her parents' home at approximately 3:00 P.M. on November 11, 1984.

Could the serial killer have kept her prisoner a
full thirteen days before actually killing her? Baker
wondered.

Forensic results showed nylon carpet fibers found on the victim's clothing matched the previous homicides. This guy had now murdered eight women. The case had completely captivated the attention of the Tampa Bay area and was just beginning to attract national attention.

That's when Lisa McVey got on her bike.

*T*he black shiny shoes that Lisa McVey wore beat a rapid tattoo on the Hillsborough County Courthouse's tiled floor. Her five-four frame looked almost thin in her white, short-sleeve shirt and forest green pants that sported a racy black stripe down the sides. Looking closer, her arms were tanned and fit.

She passed what used to be Judge Graybill's courtroom. Courthouse insiders called Graybill "the Riddler" because of his tendency to ask attorneys obtuse questions. He'd sit up there on the bench with his fingers to his cheek, his other hand leaning on the side of his chair, rocking, looking at the record of testimony playing out in front of him on a computer screen and then suddenly burst out with, "Objection sustained!" or "Objection overruled!"

Lisa McVey sat down to talk. She has a nice smile, showing off her big, white front teeth. Her light brown hair, in a pageboy cut, framed a plain face.

She remembered that night of November 3,

1984, quite well. At 2:00 A.M. she was planning her own suicide.

"I was seventeen years old and I had a job where I worked for Krispy Kreme. I did all the packaging and I was working late," she began in a deep voice softened by southern inflections.

" 'You want to work a double shift?' my boss would say.

" 'Sure, I'll work a double shift, I don't wanna go home,' I'd tell him."

It was no wonder.

"I worked late because I was already being abused at home," she explained. "Had been my whole life. First by my brothers, then when I went to live with my grandmother, her boyfriend. My grandmother never did anything about it. She'd sit there and watch what he'd do to me. Then a week prior to my abduction, my grandmother left me alone with him and moved out.

" 'You're seventeen now, you'll be eighteen soon, I think it's time to have a baby with you,' the boyfriend said. He wanted to get me pregnant. All I could think was, I'm not bringing a baby into the world like this! I didn't want to live. I was *sick* of it. I was tired of being abused."

The only thing McVey could imagine that would change her life was suicide. She looked down at her Krispy Kreme uniform, the white, short-sleeve shirt and khaki pants. Pulled back in a ponytail, her waist-length hair flew in the breeze as she rode her bike home.

"It was dark, a clear night. I was riding on Florida Avenue, my normal route home. The street's a mixture of suburban homes and businesses. A car drove by blowing its horn. Was I in its way? But I wasn't; I was on the sidewalk. I thought, 'Maybe I'll take a different way home tonight.' "

McVey pedaled down a rarely traveled side street.

"This dog came out and barked at me. I'm afraid of dogs, so I got really scared, turned at the next corner and came back onto my normal route. I was crossing over Rome Avenue. There's a park on one corner, and I saw a van parked parallel to it. 'That's kind of odd,' I thought. 'The front of the van is facing the wrong way.'

"Across the street is this huge church and this big parking lot in front of it. There's this red car sitting there, and I'm thinking, 'That's kind of odd. Why would a car be sitting in the middle of a parking lot at 2:00 A.M. in the morning?' And no sooner had I thought that then this guy jumped out at me.

"The van was somebody else's. It had just broken down and he used it to hide behind. Someplace in the shadows. Just as I was going by, he stuck his forearm out and knocked me off my bike."

In the NFL, they call it "clotheslining." Bobby Joe Long was a huge football fan.

"Suddenly, I was on the ground. He got me from behind with his arm around my neck. He puts this gun to my head. Fear . . . I just had a sense of fear. My second instinct was, 'I'm going to survive this attack.' I guess I said that because I was already surviving this kind of stuff for years."

She screamed to attract attention.

"He shouted at me to shut up. I said, 'Okay. Whatever you want I'll do. Just do me a favor.'

" 'What's that?' he screams back.

" 'Just don't kill me.' When you feel the cold barrel of a gun to your left temple, you tend to kind of work with the person.

" 'You gotta show me a good time tonight,' he says.

"Then he drags me across the street and puts me in the same red car that had distracted me earlier. My eyes are open. I see the spoked wheels, the white seating, and the *red carpet* on the floor. Everything I could remember, I remembered.

"Then he ordered me to strip down to nothing. I took off my clothes, then my bra and panties. I'm naked, and then I had to perform oral sex on him in the parking lot. When he didn't ejaculate, he had me stop.

" 'Oh, you've done this before?' he says. 'You have a boyfriend?'

"I'm thinking, 'Great! Now I need to lie to this guy.' I didn't tell him I didn't have a boyfriend or that I was being abused at home. He probably would have used that, figuring he'd abuse me worse. So I lied. I told him I *had* a boyfriend.

" 'Your boyfriend's a lucky man. Look, we're gonna take a ride. Lay back in the seat.'

"Then he blindfolded me. It was with a pre-torn strip of linen, taken from a sheet with a flower pattern. When he put the blindfold on my head, I tightened my jaw so when I relaxed later the blindfold would be a little loose and I could maybe see. He used other strips to restrain my arms and legs.

"The window was down while he was driving, I got the sense of direction he was going in. Soon as he hit the interstate, the wind changed. You know how when you're sleeping in the car and someone else is driving, you see those fluorescent streetlights going by even through your eyes are closed? It was like that.

"I peeked a little under my blindfold. There was a green digital clock. And there, on the dashboard, in shiny, silvery letters, it said 'Magnum.' I remembered Magnum specifically because I used to watch *Magnum PI*. From then on, everything I looked, touched, felt, smelled, I related it to something I would remember. If I ever got free, I knew I could help the police catch this guy."

Driving for only about twenty minutes, McVey knew they were still someplace in the county.

"Then, he stopped. I thought, 'This is it, he's gonna rape me, he's gonna kill me.' He told me to get dressed. Before I did, he got out of the car. You gotta understand, I also had my period. Last thing I wanted to do is if he raped me, have that tampon go up inside me and injure me inside so I couldn't have kids. I turned so he wouldn't see me, pulled it out and put the tampon with my blood under the car seat. If they found me dead, at least someone would know I was trying to survive."

And it could also help identify her if her body were never found.

"He gets me out of the car. My pants are ripped on the left side, from when he pulled me off the bike. I'm walking straight; he's got the gun in my back. I peeked under my blindfold for a second. We were walking toward a duplex strip mall with maybe six or seven stores. Above them were apartments.

"I felt this handle. We'd gotten to a door. I felt cold glass panes against my palm. He opened the door and we walked up these carpeted stairs. The carpet was green, with red and yellow spots or dots in it. I wanted to see if he was left- or right-handed; don't ask me why. He kept always grabbing me with his left hand. It was white. And whenever he could, he held the gun in his left. So I figured he was a left-handed white guy.

"He stops and opens this door. I could smell new paint. I figured the apartment had recently been painted. He took off the blindfold but told me to keep my eyes shut. He ordered me to get undressed and step in the bathtub.

"He gave me a shower."

McVey's voice strained higher in incredulity.

"He was holding me while he bathed me, and washed my hair. He told me to make sure my eyes stayed closed, but I opened up for a second. He had brown hair. Still couldn't see his face. Pissed me off I couldn't see his face! He made me get out of the shower and dry my hair with a hair dryer. That's when he started to rape me continuously for the next thirty-six hours . . . he raped me for thirty-six hours," McVey's voice repeated, her voice lowering an octave.

"He starts by throwing me on the bathroom floor and mounting me. He pounds away and then he realizes I'm on my period. 'Fuck! Goddamn! Why didn't you tell me you had your period?'

"Right then and there, I thought he was gonna kill me. And I didn't say anything, but he kept raping me. Didn't seem to matter to him. After a while he made me stand up and go into the bedroom—I guess that's what it was because that was where the bed was—and he had me stand facing a wall.

"Well, I still don't have the blindfold on yet. I'm telling you, it is so dark in this apartment! It was *so* unbelievably *dark*! I'm standing naked, staring at a wall; I've got my eyes open.

" 'Shut your eyes.'

"I could see a fan in the room; I could see a picture on the wall. He's got the gun raised to my back; I could *feel* it. He tells me to get in the bed, he guides me to bed, so I fall, how nice, and I get in the bed, I'm crying.

" 'Don't cry, I'm not gonna hurt you, it's okay, we're just gonna have a good time.'

"Somewhere down the line I must have gained his trust because I hear the sound of bullets falling into a drawer. He was emptying his gun, one bullet at a time." That meant it was a revolver. "He blind-folded me again and raped me. I kept thinking:

" 'I can't believe this is happening, why me, why me, why me . . . ?

" 'Is he gonna kill me?

" 'What's my family gonna do without me?' I have three brothers and a twin sister.

" 'Will I ever graduate from high school?

" 'Will I ever get married?

" 'Am I ever gonna have a *life*?'

"One time he woke up in the middle of the night and asked me about my boyfriend. I lied about who he was and what he looked like. There was no boyfriend.

" 'Do you have P.E. [physical education] in school?' he asked.

" 'Yes sir I do.'

" 'Describe to me what the girls look like naked.'

"And I had to make up stories because when I went to P.E., I never dressed out; that's typical when a child gets abused. I always dressed privately in the bathroom stall. So I made up what the girls looked like, some sort of fantasy I spun. Then I asked him:

" 'Why are you doing this to me? You don't even know me."

Long told her, "I had a bad relationship. A girl broke off with me and I'm gettin' back at women in general. Don't take this personally."

"Right. I lost track and didn't know what time it

was until he put on the TV and *Airwolf* was on. So I knew it was Friday night at eight o'clock because that's when the show came on."

Then a news bulletin interrupted the show.

" 'Seventeen-year-old girl missing, feared dead, may be victim of . . .'

"He immediately turned the TV off. I started to cry; I still had the blindfold on.

" 'Please don't cry,' he said. 'I'm not gonna hurt you.'

" 'You're already hurting me.'

" 'Well I don't want to have to get more violent with you. Here, try to eat.'

"He gives me a sandwich and a Coke. I hate soda, the smell and taste of it. But I took a little sip and then thought, 'What if he's put some kind of poison in it?' And the sandwich, I couldn't eat. Then he continues to rape me after that and about three o'clock the next morning he gets up. I've been awake the whole thirty-six hours.

"He asks me, 'What do you think I should do with you?' When he asked that question, I knew I had some leverage; I was gonna use it.

" 'I will be your girlfriend,' I told him. 'I won't tell anyone what happened to me. I will take care of you.'

" 'Oh, I can't keep you here, I can't take that chance!'

" 'Okay, then, you can take me home. Can you take me home? I have a sick father at home. He's not ready to live life without me. I take care of him all day long. I even quit school to stay home and take care of him and now you're taking me away from my father.'

" 'Well, what area of town do you live in?'

"I told him, 'Wellwood, near Hillsborough and Rome Avenues.'

"Still blindfolded, he takes and puts me back in the Magnum and takes off. 'Where's Rome Avenue?' he asks after driving awhile.

" 'Where are you now?'

" 'I'm at Mendenhall.'

" 'Well, you passed Rome.'

" 'Son of a bitch, muthafucker,' he screams. 'I can't believe we passed the street!'

" 'Look, it's all right, just turn around, Rome is the next street up at the traffic light there.' He turns around and drives into a parking lot behind a strip mall business. And then he turns to me.

" 'I know you're gonna go to the police, I wish you wouldn't,' and he hugs me. *He hugs me.* 'But just tell them that I'm black, that I'm real nasty, and please tell your father I hope he feels better. Take care of your father. For me.'

"He gets out of the car and opens the door for me. He takes me over in front of this tree. 'I want you to stand here for five minutes so when I leave you don't see my car.' I say 'Okay,' and he takes off. I'm standing there, still blindfolded, and I'm thinking, 'I wanted to get his license tag.' I pulled the blindfold off and ran into the street. Too late. He was long gone.

"I knelt down by the tree and started crying. I'm thinking, 'What if this guy figures he made a fatal mistake and comes back for me?' I ran and I ran and I ran. It seemed like it took forever to get home. The only reason I went back home was I knew in my heart that my grandmother would be there. Lo and behold she was! Her boyfriend had called to tell her I was missing.

"I'm scared out of my mind. I couldn't believe what I just went through. Did I imagine it? Did it really happen? Oh yeah, it really happened. But when I got home, my grandmother's boyfriend beat the shit out of me!

" 'You're screwing around on me,' he screamed, and all kinds of stuff. It was awful. Five hours later, my grandmother told her boyfriend, 'Enough's enough,' and she called the police."

Lisa McVey came home in the early morning hours of November 4, 1984. Tampa PD called Pops Baker in Hillsborough Homicide and told him about McVey's escape. Could this be their guy? Baker urged the Tampa Police Department to send their rape evidence to the laboratory, and on November 13, 1984, the laboratory called with the biggest break yet in the serial murder case: they found the same red fibers on McVey's clothes as had been found on the homicide victims.

"It was during my first of what turned out to be numerous interviews that they linked my abduction and rape to the murders they were investigating," McVey recalls.

Consisting of the Hillsborough County Sheriff's Office, the Tampa Police Department, the Florida Department of Law Enforcement, the Pasco County Sheriff's Office, and the Federal Bureau of Investigation, a task force was formed the next day.

"I remembered that after leaving his apartment where I was held, before he let me go, he stopped at a twenty-four-hour teller machine to withdraw some money," Lisa continued during one of her many police interviews.

Based on the time he dropped her off and backtracking, the cops figured that he was at the cash machine about 3:00 A.M.

"His car was red with a red carpet. I also remembered that while doing that, I glanced up. We were on the interstate. And saw a Howard Johnson's motel as we drove up on the interstate. But what I remembered most vividly was peeking under my blindfold at the word 'Magnum' on the dash.

At this time, there were approximately thirty officers assigned to the task force. They immediately flooded the North Tampa area searching for the apartment and vehicle. Only a 1978 Dodge Magnum has the word Magnum on the dash. A task force member was flown to the state capital and returned with a list of every Dodge Magnum registered in Hillsborough County. An examination of the computer printout of these registrations revealed Robert Joe Long's name as a listed owner of a Dodge Magnum.

Each team of detectives was assigned certain areas to search, and as one team drove to their area, they noticed a red Dodge Magnum driving down Nebraska Avenue in North Tampa. The vehicle was stopped, and the driver was told that they were looking for a robbery suspect. The driver, identified as Robert Joe Long, was photographed and a field interrogation report was written. Then they let him go.

It was brilliant strategy, and it bought time.

While the cops built their case against Long, the task force began twenty-four-hour surveillance, also using aircraft to minimize the chances that Long would spot the surveillance teams. During this same time period, bank records for all bank machines in North Tampa were subpoenaed. They revealed that Long had used the twenty-four-hour teller machine close to his apartment at approximately 3:00 A.M. on the morning Lisa McVey was released.

"Three different times," McVey recalled, "I had to go down to the police station to help make a sketch of this guy. The description I gave the police matched what Long looked like. I know I was blindfolded, so how did I see his face? Through my hands.

"He took my hands when we were in the bed and put them on his face. That was when he told me why he was raping me. His pockmarked face, his small mustache, I memorized what he looked like. He was a very clean-cut boy. His jaw was very hard.

"They took six photographs of these guys and put them on the table. Baker asked me if I could pick out the guy. I looked down at the pictures and saw him there, right in the middle. I picked up Long's picture and told Baker, 'This is the guy.' "

Based on McVey's statements, both an arrest warrant and a search warrant were drawn up and approved by a circuit court judge. Approximately two hours after being stopped by the task force members, Bobby Joe Long sauntered out of a movie theater in North Tampa, where he was arrested and returned to his apartment. Fifteen detectives were waiting there for his arrival.

In Hillsborough County they prefer to execute a search warrant while the owner of the property is there to witness the search. In this case, an embarrassed Long refused to exit the police vehicle and witness the search. Long was then taken to the HCSO operations center for interrogation.

The officers opened the interview by carefully talking only about the McVey rape and abduction, until Long confessed to being McVey's abuser. Then the detectives began going into the other homicide cases. Long initially denied any involvement in the homicides.

Meanwhile, his car had been brought to the Sheriff's Office where it was being searched. Matching tire evidence from the homicides, his car was found to have the Vogue tire and the Goodyear Viva tire, all with the white walls inverted and in the exact location on the vehicle as suspected.

A sample of the carpet was removed from the vehicle, and an FBI fiber expert on call was immediately flown with this sample and previous fiber samples to the Florida Department of Law Enforcement lab in Sanford, which had a comparison microscope. A short time later the agent telephoned Baker, confirming that the fibers from Long's vehicle matched the red carpet fibers found on all the previous victims.

Long continued to deny committing the murders. Baker then explained to him the significance of the matching fibers and what other comparisons would be done—the hair, blood, etc.

Why not continue to keep his mouth shut? Like many serial killers, Long was a braggart. Confronted with evidence of his criminal "brilliance," he gave police a brief description of each homicide. He also admitted killing Loudenback, victim number three, who was not previously linked to him. As Long told police how he murdered and raped the women, McVey arrived home from the station.

"My grandmother's boyfriend tried to rape me. I told him, 'If you touch me, I *will* kill you. I will take a gun to your head and *kill you*. No one is ever going to touch me this way again.' "

After that, the boyfriend left her alone.

Back at the HCSO, Long was telling the cops

how he used the same con man M.O. in every murder. He would talk the victims into his vehicle, immediately gaining control of them with a knife and gun. He then bound them and took them to various areas where he sexually assaulted and then murdered them.

Long drew a map showing where he had placed victim number nine. This victim had been abducted from the city of Tampa during an earlier part of the investigation, and the Tampa Police Department had informed the HCSO of this fact. They believed she fit the "victim profile," but she remained missing until Long told them where to find the body.

By spring 1985 the state was ready to go to trial. Long's first trial, for murdering Virginia Johnson, was held in Dade City, Pasco County, on April 22, 1985. It lasted a week, received a great deal of media coverage, and at the end of it, Long was found guilty and sentenced to die in the electric chair.

The state of Florida is nothing if not practical. They decided to try the Michele Simms case because of the brutal nature in which she had been killed; and the Karen Dinsfriend case because it contained the strongest forensic evidence. Then the state decided to plead out the rest of the murders. After all, how many times could you fry a guy? Electricity costs a lot of money.

As a result of discussions between the Hillsborough County State Attorney's Office and the Public Defender's Office of Hillsborough County, a plea bargain was agreed upon for eight of the homicides and the abduction and rape of Lisa McVey. In return for a sentence of life, Long pleaded guilty on September 24, 1985, to all of these crimes. In addition, the state retained the option to seek the death penalty for the murder of Michele Simms, which they did in July 1986, when Long was found guilty of her murder. During the penalty phase before imposing sentencing the judge and jury got to consider the mitigating factors. In Long's case there were quite a few.

When he was five years old, Long fell from a swing and was knocked unconscious, his right eyelid skewered by a stick. It left him with the right lid higher than the left. This was the first of six concussions he suffered due to a variety of accidents before he was ten years old. It didn't help matters that by twelve, Long had been in numerous car accidents that also left him with a malformed jaw, or that he had grown breasts, which his friends teased him about unmercifully.

Bobby Joe Long was a mutant, an "XX boy." Like most boys in his situation, he had remained undiagnosed for Klinefelter syndrome. Occurring in one out of six hundred births, KS boys like Long have two X chromosomes and one Y, instead of the sex's normal XY complement. In puberty, KS boys develop breasts. Long also displayed another KS hallmark—decreased testicular size.

When he was thirteen, Long had surgery to remove the excess breast tissue. He also shot his cat in the vagina. That might have been a dead tip-off to anyone in his family who was taking notice that his behavior was a bit aberrant. After his motorcycle collided with a car when he was twenty-one years old, Bobby Joe Long got even worse.

He spent several months in the hospital recovering from a severe concussion, his seventh. He also had a crushed leg, which the doctors seriously considered amputating. Luckily for Long, they didn't. But while he was in the hospital, his sex drive went into overdrive, which doctors attributed to this last concussion. From then on Hillsborough County became Bobby Joe Long's personal hunting ground.

The judge and jury in Hillsborough County didn't care. They took only forty-four minutes of deliberating before they sentenced him to die once again in "Ol' Sparky," Florida's electric chair. The electric bill *was* going up.

Long is currently housed in Union Correctional Institution at Raiford, Florida. He has been on Death Row for two decades while his appeals wind their way through the courts.

In getting Long to allow her to live, what Lisa McVey did is unprecedented. She conned the serial killer. It left her with a bitter and understandable anger toward Long, but also anger toward the criminal justice system at that time.

"After this whole thing went down, you would never know who I was. I had no victim's assistance; I had no victim's advocate to help me through the courts. Oh, I hate the courts."

And yet, Lisa McVey now serves the system that she once hated. On May 15, 2005, she stood up to her full five-foot-four-inch height. On her waist was a holster. In it was her nine millimeter automatic. On her chest was a Hillsborough County deputy's star. Lisa McVey is now a thirty-eight-year-old rookie deputy sheriff for Hillsborough County.

"I wanted to become a cop years ago but I needed to heal. See, I got pregnant and married at nineteen. My husband ended up being abusive to me. It's very true. When you're raised in an abusive dysfunctional home . . . my mother was a typical drug addict prostitute who would go to work one day and not come home for four months. My oldest brother would take care of us.

"The sexual abuse by my brothers happened at such a young age, I repressed it until I was an adult. What had happened was one of my mother's husband's was making my brothers do things to me and my sister."

She remembered nothing until, "I had a nightmare one night a couple of years back, woke up crying, thinking 'What the hell!' I called my oldest brother and I asked him and he got very quiet on the phone.

" 'There's something I need to tell you. I hope you are sitting down.' It wasn't his fault. He was a victim of abuse too. We all were. Everybody in my family was a victim of sexual abuse, and I find out later that my own mother was abused by my grandmother, the one that had the boyfriend. She actually abused my mother sexually, her and my mother's father."

McVey thinks her mother is alive, but she hasn't spoken with her in ten years. "She has nothing to do with the family. My grandmother died about seven years ago. Before she died, I was able to forgive her for what she let that man do to me. If I didn't forgive her, it would have killed me for the rest of my life."

"How about Bobby Joe Long?" I asked. "How do you feel about him?"

"MMM . . . I don't know. I want him in the electric chair, it's going on twenty-one years now and they haven't even electrocuted him."

It was a distinct way of empowering herself that McVey decided to become a police officer. Working in the parks and recreation department as a recreation leader, the athletic McVey had a conversation one day with a supervisor.

"You ever thought about being a cop?" the supervisor asked.

"Excuse me?"

"I just want to let you know that I don't know you very well but you seem to have the mentality to be a cop one day."

Other people kept telling her she should become a cop. But the timing was off until her child was

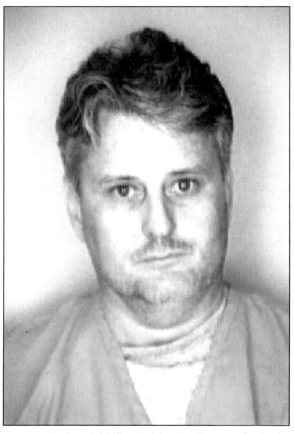

*C*onvicted serial killer Bobby Joe Long as he looks today while awaiting his execution date.

Photo courtesy Hillsborough County Sheriff's Office

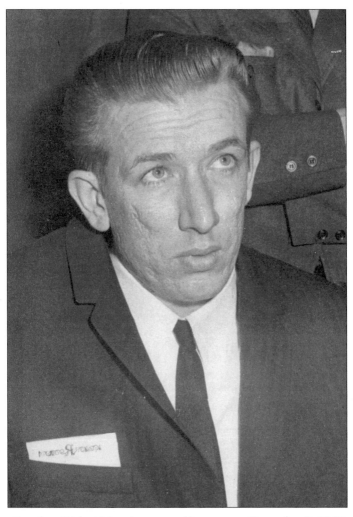

$\mathcal{W}$ hen Richard Speck appeared in court on December 9, 1966, AP photographer Paul Cannon captured this striking portrait of the killer.

Corazon Amurao on a trip back to the Philippines in 1969.

Bettman/Corbis

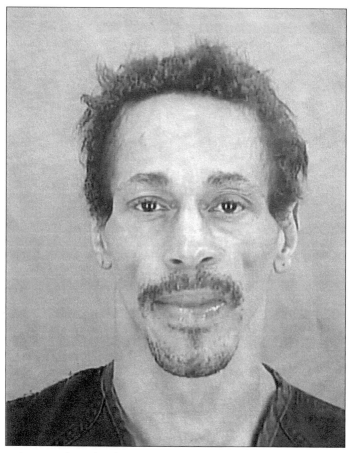

*T*racy Edwards, the only survivor of Jeffrey Dahmer, as he appears in one of his many mug shots.

Courtesy Waukesha County Sheriff's Office

On July 25, 1991, Jeffrey Dahmer appeared in Milwaukee County Circuit Court where he was charged with four counts of first-degree intentional homicide. Other counts would later be added.

*N*ita Neary, circa 1978, as she looked when she saw Ted Bundy in her sorority house.

*N*ita Neary's sorority sister Kathy Kliner DeShields, one of two survivors of Ted Bundy's bloody rampage at the Chi Omega sorority house, testified at Bundy's trial that she could not identify her assailant.

*T*ed Bundy on his FBI "Most Wanted" poster.

*K*evin Bright in his Livingston, Texas, apartment.

Photo by author

*F*rom serial killer key chains featuring the Milwaukee Cannibal and Son of Sam, to card designer Robb Moser's best-selling humor card designed around BTK's mug shot, serial killer paraphernalia is readily available on the net. Its popularity says something more broadly about American culture's fascination with exploitation, and how anything, including sociopathic killers, is grist for commerce.

Courtesy Robb Moser, Moser Studios

*C*arl Denaro, taken in Floral Park, New York.

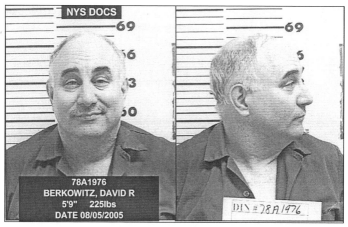

*D*avid Berkowitz, the killer who terrorized New York City in 1976-1977.

older. During that time, she healed and learned to stand up for herself.

When her daughter was old enough to be more on her own, "I just decided one day, why not?" She applied for a job in police dispatch and got it. After five years in police dispatch, she became a reserve deputy. McVey knew a lot of the brass there because of her involvement in the Long case, and she networked her way into the police academy.

On the afternoon of May 15, 2005, Deputy Lisa McVey attended the high school graduation of her nineteen-year-old daughter. She has the answer to most of the questions that buzzed through her mind during those thirty-six hours. For me, a few still need answering.

What would have happened if that dog had not caused her to change her route home that night? Would she have pedaled home on an alternate route and avoided the trap being set for her? If she had, would she have then killed herself, as she was planning prior to her abduction?

"It was really weird because when he abducted me, it was by a church parking lot and he dropped me off across the street from *another* big church.

"Years later, after I was divorced, raising my daughter on my own, one day I drove by my old complex where I lived at the time. Lo and behold, I lived between two churches."

McVey, now a Pentecostal Christian, points out, "You know, it's strange: one bad tragedy got me out of the other one. To take my own life, I was okay with that. But I was not going to allow somebody else to kill me.

"God's always been there for me. No matter what."

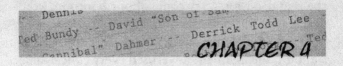
Survivor: Nita Neary
Serial Killer: Theodore "Ted" Bundy

"One second more and I [would have been] totally
in his view."
—Nita Neary

*O*nce, on assignment across the interior of Jamaica,
the six-seater I was flying in hit a bad thunder-
storm. Everyone on that plane expected to die except
the pilot and the old woman behind me, who grasped
her rosary and muttered a prayer. I remembered that
on the flight from Florida to Louisville. It was stormy
or bumpy or whatever you call it when the plane
moves up and down and your stomach with it. It was
therefore a relief to land on solid ground once again.

Louisville's airport was as lively as New Orleans
had been dead. Just in the terminal alone, people
looked more secure, more prosperous. There was a
big sign on the way out of the terminal that had Louisville's mayor smiling and welcoming you to his city.

"Thanks," I said—and strolled out into the cold
of a late February day! What was this, New York?

"Just hit a cold spell," shouted the attendant in the rental car lot. "Try some of our bourbon, keep you warm," he added with a big smile.

Signs all over the place, from the airport right out onto the highway, advertised every conceivable type of Kentucky bourbon. It is heretical to be a scotch drinker in Kentucky.

One thing both cities had in common besides being in the South was price gouging. As soon as New Orleans got the power turned back on and everyone saw how little of the place was left to inhabit, the cost of real estate sky rocketed. Unscrupulous speculators began to charge outrageous rates for rentals simply because such spaces hardly existed afterward.

In Louisville the opposite was true, with gouging the result of prosperity. It was Farm Machinery Week in Louisville. Rental cars were at a premium. Thirty dollars a day economy cars were going for $65, *if* you were lucky enough to get one.

"Supply and demand, you know," said the rental car agent with a wink. More like piracy, I thought, with the agent playing the part of Long John Silver.

The airport is on the outskirts of the city, and it took a few minutes of driving before the city of Louisville lit up the darkness like a roulette machine. Louisville has an astonishingly modern, clean skyline of varying colors and light schemes. Yet, there is something of the grandeur of the old South about the place, but with its modern roots firmly planted in the twenty-first century.

Unfortunately, because it was Farm Machinery Week, the only available hotel room was in Clarksville, across the Ohio River over a rickety-looking bridge that Daniel Boone might have crossed. After checking into the hotel, a pleasant surprise awaited—a southern buffet complete with ribs, fried chicken, and scalloped potatoes. Downing two Lipitors, I dug in with relish.

"Is food always so good in Kentucky?" I asked the waitress between mouthfuls.

"I wouldn't know," she laughed. "You're in Indiana."

I had forgotten that the Ohio River separates Kentucky from its sister state. Finishing dinner, I crashed in my room. Opening a battered leather satchel I took out an old newspaper clipping from 1978 and placed it on the bed.

STUDENT SAYS BUNDY FLED
MURDER SCENE IN FLORIDA;
COMPLAINTS ABOUT JAILERS

MIAMI, July 17 (AP)—With a slight scowl on her face, a college student today pointed to Theodore R. Bundy as the man who fled the Chi Omega sorority house the night two women were killed and three others clubbed senseless.

The college student's name is Nita Neary. It was her testimony that put Ted Bundy in Florida's electric chair. She had never spoken about what really happened the night she made the acquaintance of the twentieth century's most infamous serial killer. We arranged to meet at a restaurant on the main street of the town she lived in.

The first sight of Nita Neary was surprising. She had looked bigger and brunette in press photographs than while sitting alone on the busy restaurant's couch reading a local throwaway paper. Now she's a petite blonde who keeps slim by running four miles a day.

When she smiles, showing perfect white teeth, Nita's face turns incredibly warm and beautiful. There is something about her features, like an innocence frozen in time, layered with fear and self-doubt and finally, acceptance. Her handshake was firm and dry.

"Southern Comfort Manhattan," I ordered when we got to our corner table.

This time the waiter didn't bat an eye. But when it arrived it had not been strained correctly, leaving ice floating on the top. Neary went with a chardonnay. It wasn't that she was nervous about talking, but something else I couldn't quite define.

*t*o the media that lionized his every statement and pose, Ted Bundy popularized the archetype of the handsome, intelligent, serial killer that film and television later appropriated. Bundy knew how to manipulate the media to tell the story he wanted told. What got lost was that his real bril-

liance was his exploitation of the interstate highway system.

By familiarizing himself with the roads of the
Pacific Northwest, he was able to literally speed
from one crime scene to another when he had to,
over open, unguarded roadway. Even when he
subsequently escaped from custody, he was still
exploiting the interstate system. He found ways
to slip through dragnets and drive thousand of
miles to Florida to commit murder three more
times.

Nobody starts out to be a serial killer, even Ted
Bundy. Born in Burlington, Vermont, on November 24, 1946, a bastard when people really cared
about the meaning of the word, his name at birth
was Theodore Robert Cowell. His Air Force vet-
eran father Lloyd Marshall was never in the boy's
life and had nothing to do with him. Ted's unwed
mother, Eleanor Louise Cowell, twenty-one years
old, relied on her family. She moved with baby Ted
back to her parent's home in Philadelphia.

To protect her virginity, Eleanor raised Ted to
believe she was his older sister, and his grandparents were his parents. Ted moved with his "older
sister" Eleanor to Tacoma, Washington, in 1950 to
live with relatives.

Shortly after the Washington move, Eleanor
changed Ted's surname to "Nelson." One year
later she married for the first time, to a cook named
Johnnie Bundy. Eleanor went back to the county
and changed Ted's name once again. From then on

he was known as Ted Bundy. It wouldn't be much of a stretch to say that by changing their legal names, twice in one year, Ted might have been feeling a touch of schizophrenia. Johnnie Bundy tried to ingratiate himself with his new stepson but without success. Soon, however, they turned into the Bundy Bunch.

Eleanor and Johnnie had four kids. With four siblings, young Ted spent much of his time babysitting after school. A shy sort of kid, he was picked on by the school bullies. It was a little easier for him in high school, where his intellect began to blossom. Always an above average student, and an avid skier at Woodrow Wilson High School, he plunged his considerable intellect into studying politics.

Bundy later told authors Stephen G. Michaud and Hugh Aynesworth, who interviewed him extensively: "My social life was a big zero. I spent a great deal of time with myself. It was lonely for me . . . I didn't feel socially adept enough. I didn't feel I knew how to function with those people. I felt terribly uncomfortable."

In 1965, Ted Bundy graduated from high school. That fall he began studying at the University of Puget Sound on a scholarship. Like many new freshmen who don't know what they want to do, he took a variety of courses, including psychology. It took him only two semesters to get bored. He transferred to the University of Washington in Seattle. There, he met the girl of his dreams.

Paula Holden was Ted's dream girl. From a

wealthy California family, she was also practical. She never loved Ted the way he loved her. She could see he had no real motivation in life. When Paula graduated first from the University of Washington in 1968, she told Ted "adios" and took off. She needed a more mature man for a husband.

Most criminologists, profilers, authors, and others who studied him, contend that the incident that triggered Bundy's homicidal rages was this breakup, which he allegedly never recovered from. He then took out the rage he felt toward his former girlfriend on the women he killed. This kind of Freudian voodoo fails to explain why twenty million other guys go through the same experience and don't go out and commit serial murder.

This wasn't a George Lucas movie. Bundy was not a normal human being who got turned to the "dark side" by a girl jilting him. That Bundy *seemed* depressed to people after the breakup, that he *seemed* obsessed with his old lover, and that the whole episode *seemed* to be the rationale for his crimes, is the truth. It probably *seemed* that way to Bundy too.

Sociopaths mimic human behavior. How else can they survive in a society where once they begin to kill, that society hunts them down like Harrison Ford going after the replicants in *Blade Runner*? Sure, some remote part of Bundy may have been depressed over his failed relationship the way a normal person would. But no one can say with any reliance on proven fact that prior to his being jilted, he didn't already have the twisted urges to want to brutally rape, mutilate, and finally kill women.

A more relevant question might be: how much can a budding serial killer be pushed into that existential place where he makes the decision to kill and kill again?

After his breakup with his dream girl, Bundy did what many do in similar circumstances—he hit the road. No place to lose yourself like on the open road. Determined to investigate his origins, he traveled cross-county on the interstates to Burlington, Vermont. There, he found county records that showed Eleanor was really his mother, *not* his "sister" as he had been led to believe by his "parents." They turned out to be his grandparents.

Bundy took those psychic lemons and turned them into lemonade. His origins finally known, he returned to school, determined to do well this time around. If he could, maybe he would win Paula back. Paula eventually disabused Ted of that notion. Bundy didn't care. He continued to stay in contact with her while plunging on with his life.

Handsome and personable, he turned his not inconsiderable energies to politics for the Republican Party. Working on local political campaigns, Bundy was well-liked and respected by his fellow Republicans. In his personal life, he dated divorced secretary Barbara Parkes. She fell for Ted, hard. Bundy, though, was way beyond such mortal feelings.

In 1973, Bundy graduated from college with a bachelor's degree from the University of Washington. He had decided to study law, and was accepted at the University of Utah Law School. With his life seemingly set, with everything in front of him—a real future that he had managed to carve out despite his life's travails—he chose to throw it all away.

While continuing his relationship with Parkes, he seduced his old lover Paula Holden. He took his time, and when he finally charmed her into not only accepting him, but desperately wanting him— when she loved him most and was at her most vulnerable—he dumped her. Bundy had gotten his revenge on the woman who'd had the audacity to dump him.

Seemingly, this should have been enough. Maybe it was. Who knows? Any speculation on Bundy's motives from this point onward is fruitless. The man was an inveterate liar. Whether you believe sociopaths are born not made, or the other way around, or some combination of both, doesn't matter. Ted Bundy was ready to do something that he had fantasized about many, many times.

The last thing expected, was that I would know somebody who knew Ted Bundy's first murder victim. It turned out that Chris Coburn, a friend of mine from USC's film school, knew Lynda Ann Healy well. In 1974, long before Chris and I studied film, he was the drive-time DJ on WTFA in Salem, Oregon.

"I used to give the ski report for the Northwest," said Chris. "Every day, I talked with Lynda Healy.

She worked in Seattle for the Northwest Ski Operators Association. Lynda would give me the ski conditions for my report.

"That Friday, I asked Lynda what she would be doing for the weekend. She said that she was going down to San Francisco to get together with some friends. Then she signed off, until Monday."

On Monday, January 31, 1974, Lynda failed to report to work.

"When I went to do the ski report that day, I was surprised. Lynda wasn't around. Someone was subbing for her," continued Coburn, now a high powered entertainment attorney in Los Angeles.

A quick search of Lynda's bedroom by one of her worried roommates showed that the bedspread was neat, as if the bed had not been slept in. Lynda was gone for twenty-four hours when her parents called police and reported her missing. The cops, at first, didn't think twice about it. Most missing persons reports lead to the safe return of the missing individual. It is only a much smaller percentage in which the result is different.

Performing a routine search of Lynda's bedroom for any indication as to what might have happened to her, investigators pulled down the bedspread. The sheet was soaked in blood, what the cops soon identified as Lynda's blood. Her blood-caked nightgown was found nearby. Within the next couple of months in Washington State, Oregon, and Utah, seven more women vanished under similar circumstances. Investigators from different venues made the crucial link that by virtue of the M.O. and other factors, all the disappearances were related. Pooling their information, they found a common denominator.

During many of the incidents, witnesses noticed a well-built, handsome man behind the wheel of a VW bug. Sometimes he was wearing a cast on his arm or leg. Several women who had been approached by him recalled him mentioning his name was "Ted."

It wasn't until August 1974 that the fate of two of the missing girls was sealed. The bodies of Janice Ott and Denise Naslund were found about four miles from Lake Sammamish in Washington State. From the condition of the bodies, it was clear the women had been violated sexually, and in a particularly brutal manner.

On November 8, 1974, in Salt Lake City, someone driving a VW bug and fitting the description of "Ted" tried to kidnap eighteen-year-old Carol DaRonch from a local mall. DaRonch resisted and managed to fight the guy off from dragging her into the bug. The guy drove off, but not before DaRonch got a good look at him and the car he was driving, which she quickly passed on to police.

Around the same time in Bountiful, Utah, a seventeen-year-old girl, Debby Kent, disappeared. She'd been attending Viewmont High School. A witness later told police a tan VW bug drove off quickly from the high school parking lot where it had been parked.

Four months later, in Colorado, four more women vanished from their homes and families. A month afterward, one of the Colorado four finally turned up as a decomposing corpse close to her abduction site. Like the other victims, her autopsy showed cause of death to be the result of blows from a blunt instrument. Also like the other victims, she had been brutally assaulted sexually.

That was also the case with Lynda Ann Healy. Her body turned up in the warming snows of Washington State's Taylor Mountains. Finally, on August 16, 1975, in Granger, Utah, a state cop spotted a suspicious looking man behind the wheel of a VW bug parked at the side of the road. The cop turned his spotlight on the VW. Outlined in the bright white light, he saw the car start up and take off. The cop gave chase for a few blocks when, abruptly, the VW pulled over to the side of the road.

With gun already drawn, the cop asked the guy for his driver's license. Readily handing it over, it identified him as "Theodore Robert Bundy." Without a warrant, the cop searched the bug. He found a nylon stocking, a ski mask, a crowbar, an ice pick, a piece of rope—enough to tie someone up with—and a pair of handcuffs. Wisely, the cop placed Bundy under arrest. The initial charge was "suspicion of burglary."

Bundy fit the description of Carol DaRonch's attempted kidnapper. They brought her in and she picked Bundy out of a lineup. So did other witnesses to the crime. Professing his innocence, Bundy said he knew nothing about the attempted kidnapping. As for his similarities to the "Ted" they were looking for in connection with the murders and disappearances in Washington, Oregon, and Colorado, Bundy passed it off as a meaningless coincidence.

It's SOP for suspects to be arrested and charged before the case is ready to go to trial. That way, the police take the suspected bad guy off the streets while the prosecutor builds a case. So it was that witnesses from Lake Sammamish Park came in to identify Bundy as the guy they'd noticed hanging around the neighborhood in some sort of arm or leg cast the day Janice Ott and Denise Naslund disappeared.

This time carrying court-approved search warrants, detectives converged on Bundy's Salt Lake City apartment. They found the kind of plaster of paris doctors use to make casts. Bundy had credit cards. Credit card companies were contacted. Receipts showed that Bundy had bought gas in the Taylor Mountains where Lynda Ann Healy and some of the other victims' remains had been found. It was a very strong piece of circumstantial evidence to place Bundy at the crime scenes.

Choosing to be tried by a judge rather than a jury, Bundy's trial for the aggravated kidnapping of Carol DaRonch began on February 23, 1976. Under oath, the debonair law student denied knowing or even meeting the girl. Bundy thought he had charmed the judge into believing him. The judge didn't see it that way. He found Bundy guilty and sentenced him to one to fifteen years in state prison.

With Bundy seemingly behind bars for a good, long while, on October 22, 1976, Colorado police charged him with the murder of twenty-three-year-old Caryn Campbell. Her body, battered by a blunt instrument and brutally raped, had been found on February 17, 1976. Extradited back to Colorado on her murder charges, Bundy was incarcerated in the Garfield County Jail. Having decided to be his own attorney, Bundy was given special access to the Pitkin County Courthouse library in Aspen, Colorado. He was going to show everyone what Rocky Mountain High really was.

While in the courthouse on June 7, 1977, Bundy saw his opportunity. Left unguarded in an empty courtroom, he jumped out of an open second floor window. An eyewitness who saw this improbable feat turned to a court employee who hadn't and said, "Someone just jumped out a window. Is that normal?"

Landing safely on his feet, the athlete serial killer ran half a mile down Main Street. Then he turned and hightailed it for the hills east of Aspen. Posses of sheriff's deputies and local cops fanned out into the cottonwoods and aspens that encircled the town, trying to latch onto Bundy's trail. Bloodhounds had already tracked the killer from the courthouse to the Roaring Fork River nearby. According to a group of boys who saw him, a man fitting Bundy's description forded the river.

Back in Aspen, handbills with Bundy's picture were turned out by the Sheriff's Department and heavily distributed around town. Roadblocks on all outbound highways were established. A helicopter from the Mountain Rescue Service was pulled into police service to track Bundy down.

Eight days later two sheriff's deputies stopped the stolen car Bundy was driving, a 1966 Caddy. Arrested unarmed, he was returned to the Aspen courtroom in shackles and manacles; he was arraigned before Judge George Lohr on escape, burglary, and theft charges.

What Bundy had done after going into the Aspen Hills was go south to Castle Creek, about ten miles away. He found a deserted cabin that became his hideout for the next few days. He even heard the search helicopter overhead, looking for him. When he finally left the cabin, he carried a .22 caliber rifle that someone had carelessly left behind. He left a note on the window he had broken to get in:

"Tom, sorry, broke this while putting in plywood. Will have another put in immediately. AMY."

Bundy may have fancied himself a wit, but he was no rifleman. When the weapon got too heavy to carry, he simply chucked it. Undeterred, he concocted a new escape plan from the Garfield County Jail. Over a period of six months he dieted off thirty pounds. On December 30, 1977, Bundy had shrunk himself enough to fit through a hole in the ceiling of his jail cell that had been meant to give access to the light fixture.

Inside the ceiling, he found a crawl space and followed it into a closet in the jailer's flat. When he was certain no one was around, Bundy casually walked out of the closet and the front door. Fifteen hours later the Garfield County Jail finally figured out that Ted Bundy was missing. He had escaped . . . again.

Bundy hitchhiked his way to Chicago, where he did what many a felon in colder climes does in the winter—he took a plane to sunny Florida. By then the cops had absolutely no idea Bundy had gotten an apartment in Tallahassee, right near the campus of the University of Florida.

The urges started building up again, and he had no way to assuage them except to fall back on old habits.

By the time Nita Neary made Ted Bundy's acquaintance, the serial killer had displayed two basic M.O.s in killing women. The first was to simply and brutally overwhelm them by force. That is, break into their house, surprise them in their sleep, rape them, and then kill 'em on the spot, or drag 'em out and do the deed elsewhere. All that was necessary afterward was finding a good dump site.

Or, working the street, his second M.O. was to con them into thinking he was handicapped by wearing a cast on a limb and asking for their help. The vulnerable ones would help him to his VW bug, specially outfitted without a front passenger seat, and he would then pull them into the car, chain them down below seat level, then drive away and do them in.

On the night of January 15, 1978, in Tallahassee, Bundy once again chose M.O. number one. Twenty-one-year-old Nita Neary had been attending a keg party at a nearby fraternity.

"I had only had a couple of beers and I've had *a lot* more in the past," Neary told me. "It was funny all those circumstances, when you think about it. I wasn't drinking very much. I could have stayed with my boyfriend. Instead I came home."

While Bundy's lawyers would later try to show that she was drunk at the time, her level of acute observation would not be possible under the effects of excessive alcohol. That is especially true when you consider that she was drinking the kind of watered-down beer commonly found on college campuses.

"He was already inside the sorority house when I walked into the rec room. You had a code to punch in," recalled Nita Neary, sipping her chardonnay. Her eyes were intense.

"When I walked into the rec room," she continued, "there were noises. Lots of lights. Lamps turned on. It was like I heard my dad's voice. 'What are all these lights doing on? Turn out the lights, girls.' "

Neary came from a close-knit Terre Haute family of three sisters and one brother.

"So I started just taking my time. My whole physical being just s-l-o-w-e-d d-o-w-n. Something just told me to turn out some lights. That slowed me down. And then I was walking toward the foyer, which is the entryway into the house from the front.

"I literally *felt* . . . I could hear somebody coming down the steps, that I literally *felt* a hand on my shoulder that stopped me from entering the foyer. It was just a very gentle pull on my shoulder that *stopped* me. And as I looked into the foyer, that's when I saw him with a club in his hand. I stood perfectly still. He didn't see me because I'm at the door and from that angle he couldn't see me.

"The reason I never wanted to share that with anybody is that I couldn't explain the force or power that stopped me! I just know something prevented me from entering the foyer that was higher, that didn't want me there. One second more and I would have been totally in his view.

"I froze. I just froze. I could see his profile clearly from where I was standing, silent, but he couldn't see me because of the angle of the room. It looked like he was carrying a tree limb. I didn't equate it as a club. And he had something wrapped around it in the middle where his hand was."

And then the man was gone, out the front door of the sorority house and into the night. In his wake he left two of Neary's sorority sisters dead. Lisa Levy, twenty, had been raped and bludgeoned to death. Margaret Bowman, a twenty-one-year-old art history student, had been strangled. The killer had also beaten two other girls with the club and left them in critical condition. He was later identified by police as the escaped serial killer, Ted Bundy.

Am I next? Is he coming for me? Neary wondered. She went to the one place she felt she would be safe.

"I went home to my parents in Indiana."

Safety was not forthcoming.

"The reporters published my address in the newspapers. My name's *everywhere*. He knows people."

Neary's relatives worried.

"My father wrote the paper; my sister went in and just blasted the press. Everywhere I went, my address was published. I was afraid he would come to get me. It was awful and I was frightened."

Neary's concern is understandable. Bundy was like a wraith, appearing and disappearing at will. In truth, Bundy had migrated to familiar surroundings too. On February 9, 1978, Bundy abducted twelve-year-old Kimberly Leach from her high school gym in Lake City, Utah. He raped and strangled her, dumped the body and then once again hit the interstate, heading south until he hooked up with Interstate 10 someplace in the Florida Panhandle.

By then he was driving the sort of car he liked, an orange VW bug. He'd stolen both the car and the plates. On February 15 in West Pensacola, Florida, officer David Lee spotted the orange bug Bundy was driving. Lee knew his beat well, and the orange bug was unfamiliar. Running a check on the car's tags, they came up stolen. Lee flicked on the dome lights.

Bundy stepped on the accelerator, but then he thought better of it and instead braked and pulled over. Gun drawn, Lee ordered him out of the vehicle. Bundy came out and lay on the ground. Just as the cop was about to cuff him, Bundy turned to fight. A scuffle ensued. Bundy managed to get to his feet and run. Lee fired a shot at the fleeing serial killer and Bundy went down as if he were hit.

His revolver still smoking, Lee approached Bundy cautiously. Just as he came abreast of his inert form, Bundy sprang to his feet and reached for the weapon. Lee was kind. Rather than blowing Bundy's brains out, he just beat the crap out of him. Then he finally cuffed him and took him in for booking. Hopefully, Pensacola had a jail that would hold Bundy.

"This was an extremely difficult time for me and my family," Neary said. "I was anxious, jumpy, and had trouble focusing. Sleep was fleeting and the nights were particularly long. I kept my emotions to myself, as I didn't want to worry my parents, as they had been through enough.

"My parents were very protective and wanted me to continue on with work and college as soon as possible. They knew that moving ahead was the best avenue for me. They were hurting too and didn't quite know how to help me. I was often quiet and distant, as I tried to avoid feeling too deeply. I didn't want to face the realities of the murders and the loss of my own innocence."

Neary took a job in a local floral shop while she

searched for universities that would transfer the most credits from FSU.

"I preferred making deliveries rather than working directly in the shop, as it provided space and I didn't have to field questions. Time became my enemy as I struggled with the loneliness of missing my sorority sisters. I was not allowed to attend any of the memorial services, which I fully understood because of the danger involved.

"Yet, I received no closure. I did not have the opportunity to mourn the loss of Martha and Lisa with my dear friends, and I didn't have a chance to speak with Karen or Kathy [the women Bundy maimed]. I was so proud of all the girls who empowered themselves by moving back into the house and faced their horrific loss and their deepest fears and continued on with their lives."

Justice moves swiftly in Florida. In July 1978, just six months after the murders of Lisa Levy and Margaret Bowman, Ted Bundy was tried for killing them.

"During the trial, I was very naive as to court proceedings, lawyers, counselors. They appointed a counselor to me. I remember this lady with legs up to here, and sat on this table, crossed her legs and said, 'Tell me how are you feeling?' And I thought, 'You have got to be kidding if you think I am going to talk to *you*.'

"Then I learned very quickly that when you got on the stand, one of the first questions they [ask is], 'Have you been in counseling?' " She laughed at the irony. "So, then I *refused* to do any counseling because I was sooooo determined that my testimony was going to be *valid*. And nobody was gonna take it away from me. So I did it on my own."

"Did it on her own" meant navigating the legal system as the star witness, the eyewitness, against the serial killer of the century.

"They [the defense] tried to break me down again and again. They tried to make me look like a *drunk,* they tried to make me look like a *slut,* and all I could do was answer 'Yes' or 'No.' And, I played the game. The judge allowed them to ask the same questions: 'How many beers did you have?' After five hours of testimony, with a ten minute break, I broke down and finally asked the judge, 'How many times are you going to allow them to repeat the same questions?' I had to stand up for myself. Nobody would stand up *for me*. And I learned a lot that way. I learned . . . to be tough.

"So then during the trial I was on the stand—I don't know, about three hours—I broke down and started crying. On the news that night that was viewed as a ploy for sympathy. The next time I was on the stand they labeled me the ice princess," she laughs, "because I answered very matter-of-factly, and I showed no emotion. That again was my way of [laughing], 'You bastards! You're not going to break me down!' I was *young,* twenty-one in 1978," she said wistfully.

"I was born in the same decade," I joked.

Nita laughed.

"I remember almost getting back to normal, and getting called back to Florida for interviews with the cops and prosecutors. And I'd have to explain where I was working and why I was leaving," which would once again bring Ted Bundy into her personal life.

"What I wanted to say, the theme of your book, it's funny, and I'm shaking . . . it's just amazing how my body reacts . . . when, right after it happened, they got an artist and I was an artist. Again, that's where the spiritual thing comes in. Why me? There *was* a reason.

"I worked with the police sketch artist, who did the actual drawing. I didn't get to see that sketch until the trial. And after making me sound crazy, you start to *feel* like you're crazy. Like your testimony is off base and you start to question what you saw, questioning everything, and he showed me the sketch. And I'm like, 'Hellloooo!!! This is pretty damn good!' I thought it was *really* good."

"Because of your art background?"

"I think so! And because it was so *fresh*. I just *saw* him clearly. I remember working with the artist and he couldn't get the nose right. We worked together until I was satisfied. Seeing the sketch again at the trial calmed me down. Because I thought, 'Hey, you're not crazy!'

"I wondered time and time again sitting on that stand, who was on trial? My mother kept a folder of pictures. I guess she'd shown me a couple before I got to see the lineup [which included Bundy].They

made her go on the stand and accused her of per-
suading me to say it was him. My mother was shaking and I'd get pissed, pissed as hell! Why are you
putting her through that? I was *so mad*. 'Do it to
me! You can ask me whatever you want to ask me.
You can make me look whatever you want to make
me look like, but do not intimidate my mother!'

"And this is why I don't talk to writers. If they
can't find me, they call her. I can't protect her. She
protects me," and she laughed. "She's a bull in a
china shop. But leave us alone."

She looked straight at me.

"I'm still questioning why I am talking to you. I
don't want people judging me."

"On what?"

"That an angel stopped me. I don't know if it
was an angel or . . . I don't want people judging my
testimony. It was my experience. You know, I'm a
teacher, and every once in a while somebody will
come by and say, 'I think I saw you on A&E.'

"One time, somebody's daughter went into forensics and so they had it on a [classroom] tape
that I was on the case. Her mother comes up to me
and says, 'My daughter saw you while taking this
class, can she interview you?' and I'd look at her
and go, 'Noooo!' "

Nita laughed.

"You know, it's funny because one newspaper
article said my life would never be normal, and
that's basically true. It's always going to exist. You
know what, I don't regret being involved. I don't

regret the trial; I don't regret *any* of it. And that's where the goodness of people happens. After the fog of horror lifted, what was left were good and kind people, a fierce protective family and sometimes strangers, who reached out with encouraging words, phone calls, and prayers.

"When I was ready to throw in the towel, I would get a letter from Lisa Levy's mother and it thanked me for doing what I was doing. She hoped my life would return to normal. I thought, 'I can endure this, I can stand a few hours on trial, she'll never, ever, ever return to any kind of normalcy.' "

*I*n a revolutionary effort for the time, the Florida State's Attorney's Office at Ted Bundy's Florida murder trial introduced forensic evidence that proved that Bundy's teeth matched bite marks found on murder victim Lisa Levy. Despite his best efforts to the contrary—at various times during this trial Bundy actually represented himself—the jury found him guilty.

"I bear you no animosity. But you went the wrong way, partner. Take care of yourself," said Judge Edward Cowart in sentencing him to death in Florida's electric chair.

It was in the decade leading up to his execution in 1989 that Bundy achieved his greatest notoriety. From Florida's Death Row, he was ubiquitous on news reports. He always seemed to be filing one appellate brief or another that delayed his execution time after time. Then, finally, in a last ditch attempt to avoid the chair, he began to confess to his crimes. Sometimes Bundy offered a confession to a killing quid pro quo for a death penalty reprieve. He actually had the nerve to try to con the cops into believing that he was possessed by an "entity" that had made him commit his heinous crimes.

Ever a staunch Republican of the far right, Ted Bundy morphed into an antipornography crusader. Claiming that he had been obsessed by hardcore pornography, especially involving bondage and sadomasochism, he said it had led him into ruin.

Just as Bundy was garnering headlines with his antics, Neary tried to go on with her life. But in the early 1980s in Florida there were no such things as victim impact statements or victim advocates, as there are now. Witnesses were just left to fend for themselves.

"Even after the trial, I forgave the attorneys," she told me. "I guess I didn't need to. There was nothing to forgive. Everybody just wanted to get him. I realized, basically, everybody was on the same page. They were trying so hard to get him and to follow everything through.

"You realize people like the mother who wrote me the letter, how she could just take the time, her loss was so severe. I received a lot of supportive letters from friends." She sounded so wistful. "When I was young and growing up, we played until dark and someone called you in.

"Art was always my favorite subject. I watched Jon Nagy on TV, remember him? I got his books, his charcoals, and I drew."

I nodded fondly, seeing the image of the cool, goateed Nagy who made drawing look easy on his Saturday morning baby boomer TV show, *Learn to Draw with Jon Nagy.* Surprisingly, her art did not help Nita get through this difficult period.

"I didn't use my art a lot then. The funny thing is I just shoved everything out and became really focused. It was just kind of my way of handling things. It was the way my family raised me. 'A Neary never quits.' My paternal grandfather said that, and when I'd go to trial my father would repeat it, 'Honey, a Neary never quits. I moved to northern Indiana and taught school for nine years. I got married, didn't have any kids.

"When I got divorced is when I dealt with Bundy. It was ten years later. I got so busy and wouldn't talk to anybody, and my parents were very protective. I was proving to people I wasn't a basket case.

"When I went out to student teach about a week later, the teacher was wondering about me and said, 'You're fine.' I said, 'What are you talking about?' I didn't even know he knew.

" 'Well,' he goes, 'I heard your story and thought you'd last a couple of days and then fall apart.' And I just thought, 'Don't fall apart.' " Finally, one night, "I woke up in the fetal position; I thought someone was gonna club me. I didn't sleep. I found this beautiful counselor. She was sweet and took me in.

"I let go of a lot of stuff. I would get stressed or anxious. For the first time, I felt safe telling the story. I just didn't realize how much energy it took to keep it buried. She made me see that no one was there. She taught me to meditate and silently chant my fears away."

But Bundy was ubiquitous. On February 5, 1986, Florida Governor Bob Graham signed his death warrant. The execution date was set for March 4. Once again Bundy's luck held. His execution was delayed until some legal niceties could be sorted out.

Then, Bundy's story made its way to national TV when Mark Harmon starred in a brilliant and chilling performance as Bundy in the 1987 miniseries, *The Deliberate Stranger*. It just served to burnish Bundy's reputation as the century's most notorious, and handsome, serial killer. For Neary, it was all rubbish.

"I was never interested in delving into Bundy's past or present, and I never expended any energy in following his so-called popularity with the public," she said. "My thoughts and concerns were for Martha and Lisa's families and the recovery of Karen and Kathy. Allowing Bundy to consume my thoughts would have robbed me of the time I needed to heal."

Finally, in late 1988, Bundy was all out of appeals. His execution was scheduled for early the following month. In northern Indiana, where Nita Neary was teaching at the time, it was impossible to avoid the attendant publicity.

"His execution came up and I had to face it. People would say to me, 'Hope he fries, Nita.' I felt sick. You do feel part of it."

Bundy must have read a little bit about American criminal history. In the eighteenth century it was common for the condemned to give interviews to a clergyman, admitting their guilt and praising God. Bundy did exactly that with his last interview the day before his execution. He chose Dr. James Dobson, president and founder of the far right religious lobbying group Focus on the Family. During the interview, Bundy told Dr. Dobson:

"I know people will accuse me of being self-serving, but through God's help, I have been able to come to the point, much too late, where I can feel the hurt and the pain I am responsible for. Yes. Absolutely! During the past few days, myself and a number of investigators have been talking about unsolved cases—murders I was involved in.

"It's hard to talk about all these years later, because it revives all the terrible feelings and thoughts that I have steadfastly and diligently dealt with—I think successfully. It has been reopened and I have felt the pain and the horror of that."

It was as good a con as any Bundy had ever committed.

On January 24, 1989, Ted Bundy was led to

Florida's death chamber in Starke, Florida. He sat in an upright, not uncomfortable chair made out of oak by prison inmates in 1923. The first inmate to sit in it was Frank Johnson, who was executed on October 7, 1924. Florida had a moratorium on executions from 1929 to 1979, but by the time Bundy sat down, the state was more than willing to get rid of him.

Bundy's head had been shaven in a crew cut. That facilitated the work of the electrodes, in the cap that would be placed over his head. The electrodes needed to make contact directly with his scalp. In northern Indiana at the same time, "I went to work. I gave myself the opportunity to chill," Neary remembers.

The apparatus that administered the electric current to Bundy had already been tested to ensure proper functioning. It was 7:07 A.M. when the executioner dialed up the current. It flowed through the wires, the electrodes, and into Bundy's brain. Bundy strained against the seat as the huge jolt of electricity pulsed through him. It didn't take long. When his death was announced a few minutes later outside the prison, a large crowd cheered.

Few grieved for the serial killer, but his mother did. In news accounts, Louise Bundy called Ted "my precious son." He may have actually been . . . once.

"I didn't know how I'd feel after the execution," said Neary. "But I felt relieved and sad at the same time."

In his postmortem photographs, Bundy still looked handsome, leering out from the grave. As for Nita Neary, this is who she became. It is part of her self-written autobiography for the Web site of the school she teaches in:

> *Drawing has been a part of my life for as long as I could hold a crayon. I've always been fascinated with marks and lines and how they affect a blank sheet of paper. Currently, I am working with mixed media and have shown my work in several small galleries around here.*
>
> *Teaching art to grades K-12 over the last twenty years has led me to explore and develop my own work as well as to encourage the infinite possibilities that art provides my students. Their fresh perspective and spontaneous responses to the art assignments lead to daily discoveries about their lives and their communities.*

She also became active in her community.

"I now volunteer for an organization called 'Kids-in-Court.' We help children who will testify in court become acquainted with the physical surroundings of the courtroom. The children role play, taking turns being the judge, sheriff, attorneys, and jury. They get a chance to sit in the witness chair and speak into the microphone. We hope this will educate them and ease their fears during their testimony. I know this would have helped me."

"Do you talk to your sorority friends from FSU?" I asked.

She nodded. "I'm close to my Chi Omega roommates. I've lost contact with the other sisters over the years."

*O*utside the restaurant the temperature had dropped into the high thirties. I felt that awkwardness you feel when you have accidentally stepped on someone's grave. I shivered.

"I'll walk you to your car," I said to Nita.

"Thank you."

When we got there, we shook hands warmly. I didn't know quite what to say.

"I am so glad you are alive," I said, my voice breaking hoarse, which it always does when I am filled with emotion.

"I needed him to die so I could live," said Nita. "Whether that's selfish, it is what it is."

"I'm glad *you're* alive."

Nita Neary goes on. Her grandfather and father would be happy to know that she has never quit. In fact, she won.

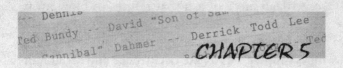
Survivor: Corazon Amurao
Serial Killer: Richard Speck

*T*he plane ride from Louisville to Chicago was less than an hour. Midway Airport was as busy as the airport in New Orleans was dead.

The car I rented came with a handheld GPS, which I thought would be helpful in checking out some street addresses where Corazon Amurao lived. Amurao had spent a lot of time dodging interviews and trying to disappear. Unfortunately, the GPS didn't come with an instruction booklet and I couldn't figure out how to use it. Relying on an old-fashioned map, feeling decidedly anachronistic and tired, I hopped on Interstate 94, which cuts right through the heart of Chicago.

July 2006 was the fortieth anniversary of the Richard Speck case, the most celebrated mass murder of the previous half century, which, not coincidentally, took place in Chicago. To anyone old enough to remember, it remains in memory like some dead piece of ash that refuses to blow away. To understand the Richard Speck case in the Millennium is to remember a quaint time, 1964, when mass murder was a rare occurrence and serial murder almost nonexistent.

Speck prepared the country for the kill totals that were about to come, except he had no cooling off period. It took him only eight hours to slaughter eight female nurses. Forget Columbine. This guy didn't hide his depravity behind automatic weapons and teenage good looks. He was a stone killer, a no good son of a bitch. Corazon (Cory) Amurao, a Filipino exchange student, was the only one to survive. The staid *New York Times* which rarely if ever would lead with such a lurid story was even impressed, bannering the story on page one:

8 STUDENT NURSES SLAIN IN CHICAGO DORMITORY KILLER TIES NINTH BUT SHE HIDES AND ESCAPES

Eight student nurses were killed here this morning in one of the most savage multiple murders in the history of crime . . .

In the story, Dr. Andrew J. Toman, the coroner, called it the crime of the century. Police Superintendent O. W. Wilson stated that in his opinion the "terrible crime" was the most shocking in Chicago's history since the St. Valentine's Day Massacre in 1929. Of course, Amurao's escape was a highlight of the article because she was the lone survivor.

Suddenly, a Filipino girl from the small town of San Luis, was the focus of every major news story in the United States. According to those early first accounts, Amurao had wiggled "free of her bonds, after she had fought down her terror . . ." Groping her way to a second story window ledge, she walked out on the precipice in bare feet.

"They are all dead! They are all dead! My friends are all dead! Oh God, I'm the only one alive!" she screamed into the early morning dawn.

*T*he seventh of eight children, Richard Speck was born the day before Pearl Harbor was attacked, December 6, 1941, in Kirkwood, Illinois. Considering the conflagration that was about to come, growing up in a small American town in the heartland with a big family doesn't seem so bad. Unfortunately, when Speck was six his father who he loved deeply, died.

He was raised by a strict Baptist mother, who restricted outside influences and alcohol. His mother made a tremendous exception to the latter rule, however, when she married Carl Lindberg, an alcoholic Texan with an arrest record. The family was uprooted to Dallas, Texas. Now the abuse really began. Speck's stepfather was the kind of alcoholic who went into rages when under the influence. That rage was frequently taken out on Speck's hide. Speck himself would become a life-long alcoholic prone to rages when drunk. He would attack the Chicago nurses in an alcoholic rage.

In the 1950s, Speck was labeled a juvenile delinquent. He got into fights, drank too much, and treated women like cattle. When he was twenty, and already drinking heavily, he figured he was mature enough to handle a marriage. Considering that he picked as his bride fifteen-year-old Dorothy Roberts, he just might have been. They had a child together, but if she ever thought she was buying into the American dream with Richard Speck, it was more like the American nightmare.

Some researcher in the early sixties claimed that men with an extra Y chromosome—XYY—composed a disproportionate percentage of America's prison population. Labeled "super males," they were thought of as violent, hostile individuals prone to criminal life. It would later be claimed by the media that Speck had the extra Y chromosome and that accounted for his deviant behavior. Scientific tests, however, showed Speck's chromosomal structure to be normal. As for the super male theory, that faded with bell bottoms.

Speck regularly beat his wife and his mother. His wife would later claim that he raped her with a knife to her throat on more than one occasion. During this period, Speck held a series of menial jobs, but nothing for too long. His stealing and burglaries kept him busy. He went in and out of jail periodically when the cops got him for one low level felony or another. Finally, in January 1966, Dorothy Speck filed for divorce from her extremely troubled husband.

Dorothy's exit turned out to be the best decision of her life. In 1966 in Dallas, Speck stabbed somebody whose apartment he then burgled. He plea-bargained the stabbing to a low level misdemeanor and was fined ten dollars. The burglary, however, would require prison incarceration, which Speck was determined to avoid at any cost. With some help from his sisters, he fled from Dallas to Chicago. He stayed with his sister there for a few days and then went to Monmouth, Illinois, a small town the family had lived in briefly when he was a child.

This seemed to be a desperate, last attempt on Speck's part to connect with his background and find some normalcy in his life. Family friends took him in. He found work as a carpenter, but that didn't last long. Quitting to engage his alcoholic tendencies, he frequented a tavern called the Palace Tap. A bartender would later remember that Speck claimed to have killed his ex-wife's husband in Dallas.

Crime in Monmouth then took a sharp spike. On April 2, 1966, Mrs. Woody Johnson was in her house when someone grabbed her from behind. The man put a knife to her throat. He told her to keep her mouth shut. He cut her housecoat into bonds that he used to tie her up. Then, when he was satisfied that she was immobilized, he raped her.

Eleven days later, on April 13, bartender Sheila Ward was found murdered. Her body was discovered in a hog house behind Mickey's One, the tavern where she worked. The autopsy showed that her liver had been ruptured by a tremendous blow or pounding to her stomach. Speck was brought in for questioning but told the police nothing. Before the cops could finish talking to him, he begged off because he felt ill. He made an agreement with the officers to return on April 19 for further questioning.

April 19 came and went and no Speck. Investigators went to his room at a local hotel. Inside was some of Mrs. Woody Johnson's jewelry. Speck liked to keep trophies; there were trinkets from many of his other burglaries.

Hours earlier a witness had seen him take off with suitcases in hand. Police would later find out that Speck got on a bus and went to Chicago.

Beginning in the 1960s, the Philippines has exported trained nurses all over the world, with the United States being her biggest customer. It has also sent more professional immigrants to the U.S. than any other country in the world, with the majority of those in the nursing profession. And Amurao—Cory, to her friends—was a nurse.

Born in the Filipino province of Batangas, south of the capital city of Manila, Amurao was a 1964 graduate of Manila's Far Eastern University Hospital. She came to the U.S. in May 1966 on what was described as "a two year exchange program." The reality was somewhat different.

Medicine was a burgeoning enterprise in the 1960s. More sophisticated medical procedures and drug developments were beginning to extend the average life span. That and other factors led to a shortage in U.S. hospitals of qualified nursing care. Americans had already begun what would become a pattern into the next Millennium of outsourcing. With American—read "white"—nurses in short supply, the hospital industry turned to the former U.S. colony, the Philippines.

Commenting on the history of Filipino nursing care in the United States, Belinda Olivares-Cunanen writes in her "Political Tidbits" column for MQ7. Net, an online Filipino news service:

> *And among the various nationalities serving American hospitals, Filipino nurses are the favorite because of their tender loving care, their facility with the language, their generally pleasant and well-scrubbed appearance, and their cheerful and uncomplaining nature (as against that of American nurses).*

> *US hospitals also prefer foreign nurses as they are able to save on salaries—in a 40-hour week of duty, the foreign nurses are paid a beginning salary of about 26 dollars an hour, versus the 35 dollars to 40 dollars an hour for US nurses. 25 dollars an hour is a lot of money for Filipino nurses, who earn much less back home, but the bigger come-on is the green card that is extended to them and their families.*

When Amurao came to the U.S., she got a job as a student nurse at South Chicago Community Hospital, on the far south side of the city. Already, many of her brethren had preceded her. This was at a time when most Americans had either a first-hand memory of Douglas MacArthur's return to the Philippines or had seen the famous newsreel footage chronicling the event.

It took the United States thirty-six years—from the time it got the islands in the Treaty of Paris ending the Spanish American War, in 1899, to 1936—to finally grant the Philippines its independence. During World War II, Japan invaded the country and defeated Allied forces led by General Douglas MacArthur. With his famous "I shall return" speech, MacArthur blazed the country's name into the minds of mainland Americans. When he turned around and followed through on his promise, reinvading in 1944—making sure, of course, that newsreel cameras were placed in the ideal spot to record the preening general stepping ashore—Filipinos found themselves embraced by their American uncle. The next time MacArthur tried that act again in Korea, Truman rightly fired him.

There were many other Filipino nurses here, having already ingratiated themselves with the Americans, so that by the time Amurao showed up, she was treated like one of the girls. She and the other student nurses lived in a town house at 2313 East 100th Street, in a nice residential neighborhood where you could walk at night and not be bothered.

On the night of July 14, 1966, Corazon Amurao was asleep in the upper bunk in one of the bedrooms in the suite she shared with the other nurses. Her roommate was in the bunk under hers. At about 11:00 P.M. they were awakened by four knocks at the front door. Sleepily, they both got up out of bed to see what was up. Amurao opened the door.

Holding a small brown pistol in his right hand was the ignorant cracker from Dallas, Richard Speck. He pushed his way in. Amurao could smell the sour alcohol on his breath. Speck herded the two women into another bedroom off the main room. Inside, four more women were asleep. They awakened to see Speck's leering pockmarked face and dark pistol. He took them all into yet another bedroom, where he yanked the sheet off the bed. Producing a knife, he used it to cut the bedsheet into strips.

"I promise not to hurt any of you," he lied. "All I want is money to go to New Orleans."

Knife at the ready, Speck sat on the floor, his rheumy eyes waiting and watching the nurses struggle to open their purses for money. One nurse handed over a five dollar bill, another four singles. After counting up his huge treasure trove, he pointed his gun barrel at each nurse, counting up how many women were in the room.

At about midnight student nurses Suzanne Farris, twenty-one, a Catholic who went to daily mass, and Mary Ann Jordan, twenty, came into the apartment. Jordan didn't live there. She was just visiting for the night.

Speck surprised them, tied them up too, and put them in the bedroom with the others.

Periodically he would lead the women one by one out of the room and into one of the other rooms in the suite. Amurao would remember hearing, "Ahhhhh . . ." sounding like stifled screams. Sometime after that she could hear him going to the bathroom and water running. He repeated that pattern all through that long night, silently coming in, each nurse knowing it was just a matter of time until it was her turn.

During one of those times he was gone, Amurao did the thing that saved her life. She rolled under the bed, all the way up to the wall. Intuitively, she was betting that Speck was lousy at arithmetic. Listening to muffled sounds from the next room, she lost all track of time.

The alarm clock went off. Still under the bed, Amurao knew that it had been set for 5:00 A.M. Therefore, it had been six hours, approximately, since the terror began. She had made a good bet.

"I thought if the man was still in the house, the alarm would scare him off," she later told police. "But I wasn't sure he had left. I waited, and when I didn't hear anything, after a while I crawled out."

Amurao had been working at her bonds until she finally pulled her way out of them. She opened the door into the main room and stepped out.

Three town houses down, Mrs. Alfred Windmiller was awakened shortly after 5:00 A.M. by noise. "I woke my husband and told him about it," she said. "He said it was a kid screaming but I told him it wasn't a child's screams."

Putting on her housecoat, Mrs. Windmiller went outside and ran in to a neighbor, Robert Hall. He was out early walking his dog. They walked three houses down and looked up. There, on a second story ledge, was Corazon Amurao, screaming.

"They are all dead! They are all dead! My friends are all dead. Oh God, I am the only one alive."

"Don't jump! Go back inside," Windmiller yelled. She began running down the street, crying for help.

Patrolman Daniel R. Kelly, twenty-five and only on the force for eighteen months, heard her cries. As he would remember it, "I called for assistance, and then went into the town house through the rear door, which was open when I got there. Then

I walked into the front room and found a body on the couch."

The girl on the couch was naked. In an astonishing coincidence, it was someone Kelly knew. Her name was Gloria Jean Davy, and Kelly had dated her five years before. Originally from Indiana, Gloria always aspired to the nursing profession. President of the Student Nurses Association of Illinois, her cause of death was strangulation with a bedsheet knotted around her throat. She was the only one of the victims that the autopsy indicated was sexually assaulted. That would make sense since Speck was roaring drunk at the time of the crimes.

Then patrolman Leonard Pomme, who'd been cruising the area in his one-man black and white, arrived on the scene. He'd been summoned by Hall, the man out walking his dog. With their forces now doubled, the two cops pulled their .38 police revolvers from their holsters and flicked off the safeties. They didn't know if the killer was still there and assumed that he was. They split up, with Pomme taking the basement and Kelly the upper floor.

"I got to the top of the stairs," Kelly recalled, "and walked past a bathroom where I found a second body. Three more were in a front bedroom and three others in another bedroom. They were strewn all over the place and there was blood everyplace."

Detectives found furniture, lamps, everything

throughout the apartment in disarray. The women had struggled and fought back, though to no avail. Detectives marked out where the bodies were found. After taking photographs of the scene and gathering evidence, the bodies were removed to the morgue, where they were autopsied.

Suzanne Farris was found fully clothed in the hallway near the second floor bedroom. The cause of death was multiple stab wounds to the chest. It is doubtful Speck allowed her to pray before executing her.

Patricia Ann Matusek, twenty, had just gotten engaged ten days earlier, on July 4. She was marrying a fellow nurse who was about to go into the Army and faced the very real prospect of being sent to attend the wounded troops in Vietnam. Matusek was determined that after she graduated in August, she'd get a job at Children's Memorial Hospital. Wearing "night clothing," she was found in the second floor east bedroom. The cause of death was strangulation with a bedsheet.

Mary Ann Jordan thought she would be going home in the morning. She didn't. Wearing "night clothing," she was also found in the second floor east bedroom. The cause of death was multiple stab wounds to the neck, chest, and eye.

Pamela Lee Wilkening, twenty, was athletic. A car racing enthusiast, she had written on her nursing application: "A nurse is supposed to help people, and I want to be someone who does this." She was wearing "night clothing" when found in the second floor east bedroom. The cause of death was multiple stab wounds to the chest. She had also been strangled with a piece of the torn bedsheet.

Valentina Pasion, twenty-three and Merlita Gargullo, thirty-three, had come over from the Philippines together. With Amurao, they comprised the Filipino contingent in the group of nurses in the town house. Pasion and Gargulla had already worked as registered nurses in the Philippines, and both women dutifully sent half of their paychecks to support their families at home.

Discovered in her night clothing in the second floor bedroom west, Pasion's cause of death was multiple stab wounds to the neck and chest. She'd also been strangled with a strip from the bedsheet. Gargullo was found in the second floor west bedroom, also wearing night clothing. Her throat was cut from ear to ear.

Nina Jo Schmale, twenty-four, was engaged to her childhood sweetheart. A volunteer at an old persons' home, she aspired to be a psychiatric nurse. Discovered in the second floor west bedroom wearing night clothing, Schmale's cause of death were multiple stab wounds to the neck. She had also been strangled with the bedsheet, with a second strip tied over her mouth as a gag. She couldn't scream.

Amurao told the police that the killer was six feet tall, blond hair, 160 pounds, with a southern drawl. Working with a sketch artist, Amurao produced this sketch of the killer:

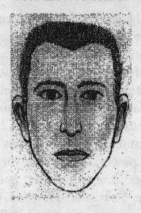

The police sent teams of detectives out on the street to canvas the neighborhood. Their initial thought was that whoever was their bad guy, he knew the neighborhood well. At a gas station a few blocks away, cops found a witness who claimed that a guy had left two bags there, and had complained because he'd lost out on a Merchant Marine job. That led the cops to the Merchant Marine Union Hall on 100th Street, walking distance from 2313 East 100th Street. There, no one had seen a seaman who matched Amurao's description. But returning to the gas station, they found a second witness who had talked to the tall blond guy. The witness had sent him to a rooming house on Commercial Avenue and 94th Street.

The cops checked that flophouse and the rest of them on the South Side and came up empty. Going back to the union hall, detectives found a shipping agent who remembered a seaman who had been angry because he'd missed a berth on a ship. Fishing in the trash, he came up with an assignment sheet that had the guy's name on it—Richard Speck.

Now the cops had a name to go with their suspect. All they had to do was find him. At that moment he was actually at a cross-town bar called Pete's Tap. When he walked in, he had a twelve-inch hunting knife dangling from his belt. Months earlier he had pawned his watch for some booze. With the nurses' money on him, Speck bought it back from the bartender. He then proceeded to brag about the people he'd killed in 'Nam with the knife on his belt.

As he got drunk, Speck got looser. He took the knife off his belt, went behind the bar and, from behind, put the knife across the bartender's throat while restraining him with his left arm across his chest. Speck claimed this was the way he killed. The bartender, unimpressed, pushed him away and told the seaman to take off. Speck turned on the charm and talked his way into staying. A regular at the bar, Bob Conrack liked the knife and bought it from Speck. The two drunken seamen, Speck and Conrack, staggered across the street to another bar, where they continued to get loaded.

At the bar, people were talking about the murders of the nurses. That's when Speck discovered, to his chagrin, that there was a survivor; he'd been sloppy, very sloppy.

"It must have been some dirty muthafucker that

done it," Speck spit out at Conrack pissed at himself that he had left one alive.

Someplace during the afternoon, Speck found another drinking companion, Simon "Says" Granger. Also from the South, Granger and Speck went on a bender. After hitting so many bars they couldn't count, Simon wanted some sleep. Speck invited him to use his motel room at the Shipyard Inn. They went there, Granger got into the bed, and Speck decided to go out for more partying.

While Speck went back out on Chicago's streets, tempting the cops to find him, the cops in turn were doing exactly that. The agent at the seaman's hall gave them Speck's sister's phone number, the number he used on his application form. The cops had the agent call the number and tell Speck's brother-in-law, Jeff Riboux, that Speck had gotten a job. He needed to ship immediately. Riboux said he would check to see where he was. Calling around, he found Speck at the Shipyard Inn.

During their conversation, Speck was told to go down to the union hall for a berth on the ship *Sinclair Great Lakes*. Speck claimed that he couldn't get there for at least an hour. But he must have sensed something was wrong because he never showed up. Instead, he packed his bags, woke up Granger, raced downstairs, and had the manager call for a cab. While waiting for it, Speck decided to play some pool in the bar.

He was watching as plainclothes detectives walked into the Shipyard Inn. He overheard them say they were looking for a tall blond guy with a southern accent. As he played pool mere feet away from his pursuers, the cops continued their conversation with the manager. Satisfied that Speck wasn't there, they went out to try the next flophouse. Speck waited until they left, then strolled. Outside, his cab had finally arrived. He got in with his bags and told the driver to go north.

Richard Speck had decided to use his sister's home as a hideout. Problem was, he didn't know where she lived. He figured she lived in a poor side of town. "You know, where all the beatniks are," he told the cabby. Not surprisingly, the cabby didn't know where to go. The only beatnik he knew was Maynard G. Krebs on "The Many Loves of Dobie Gillis." Finally, a totally clueless Speck had the cabby drop him off in front of the Cabrini-Green projects. Then he walked a few blocks down to Dearborn and checked into another flophouse, the Raleigh Hotel. The name he signed on the register was John Stayton, who was actually one of Speck's Texas friends.

Speck found a woman and took her up to his room. She came down a half hour later and told the hotel manager, "he has a revolver." Next morning, someone from the hotel called the police. Two cops from the Eighteenth District police station came over immediately. When a fully clothed Speck woke up that morning, they were looking down at him. The first thing they asked him was "Why [do you have] a gun sticking out of your pillow?"

Speck said it wasn't his, that it belonged to the black hooker he had been with a short while ago. Looking in the wallet, the cops found Speck's passport and seaman's card. Unfortunately, not every cop in Chicago was aware of Amurao's description of the killer. Nor were they all aware that the name of the suspect was Richard Speck. That included the two cops in Speck's flophouse room.

Chicago's Finest confiscated the gun of known mass murderer Richard Speck and left Speck to his afternoon's devices. That included prodigious drinking at a series of bars, a bout that went into the evening hours. But the police—the ones who were informed—were hot on his trail. They found the cabby who had picked Speck up. He told them that he'd dropped the guy at the Cabrini-Green projects. Cops showed up, armed with Winchester rifles. With this guy, they were *not* kidding around. If the Untouchables were still around in Chicago, they'd be looking for him.

Meanwhile, Speck ran into two old drinking buddies Sam "the Man" Raisch and Larry Talbot. Speck's friends were staying at a flophouse called the Star Hotel. He went back to the Raleigh and packed his bags.

"I'm going to the laundry," he told someone who asked where he was headed.

Then he checked into the Star Hotel. About fifteen minutes later detectives showed up at the Raleigh and showed the manager Speck's picture. The manager stared at it.

"It's him, it's Richard, he just left," the manager said.

At his new abode, the Star Hotel, Speck sat out on the fire escape with his drinking buddies, Sam the Man and Larry Talbot, putting away a quart of cheap wine. They talked about hopping freights. The next morning, Speck got up at dawn, ready to hop a freight and get out of town. Sam the Man, who had said he would accompany him, reneged, and Speck went off by himself to pawn some of his things for money.

By then, police had gotten a match on the fingerprints inside the town house with Speck's. It gave them airtight forensic evidence to tie him to the murders. Detectives went to the Illinois State Attorney's Office in Chicago for an arrest warrant.

While they were doing that, Speck was getting drunk again, this time picking up a pint of cheap wine at a liquor store. He saw the newspapers with his name and picture splashed across the front page as the prime suspect in the nurses' murders, and bought them, to revel in his newfound celebrity.

Until then, Speck's luck as a fugitive matched TV's Richard Kimble. It was about to run out.

Back at the Starr Hotel, he drank his wine and in a drunken stupor, he staggered into the communal bathroom down the hall. He decided it was time to check out. He dropped the bottle, then used the broken glass to cut his wrist. He was so drunk he didn't feel very much. Back in his cubicle—the Star divided up their "guest" rooms into small, filthy five-by-three-foot cubicles—Speck lay down on the bed.

His drinking buddy Sam the Man, who'd reneged on the freight-hopping trip, had taken a job as a day laborer. He was walking home after work, when he saw the papers with Speck's picture and name. Back at the Starr, he found Speck in the midst of his pathetic suicide attempt. He anonymously called the police and told them that the guy they were looking for was staying at the Starr Hotel. For some reason, the police never sent a car.

Instead, Speck was rushed by ambulance to Cook County Hospital. The nurses' bodies were at that moment cooling in the same hospital's morgue. Despite having a police bulletin with Speck's name and picture in front of them on the dash, the ambulance drivers never noticed who their celebrity patient was. Rushed into the emergency room, Speck was being prepped for surgery when a resident, Phil White, noticed the distinctive tattoo on his arm. It said, "Born to Raise Hell."

Emergency rooms in the city had a plentiful supply of the police wanted posters for Speck. White compared the man on the gurney to the mug shot from one of Speck's previous arrests in Dallas. It was the same man. Speck had started pleading for water. White grabbed him by the back of the neck, hard, and said, "Did you give water to the nurses?" White let him go, called in a cop who was guarding another patient down the hall and told him he had Richard Speck on a gurney.

The cop came in and officially captured the mass murderer, who wasn't going anyplace. Detectives were called and surrounded Speck, even as he was being prepped for surgery, and placed him under heavy guard. It turned out his aborted suicide attempt had severed an artery. The doctors were determined to fix him up nicely so he could stand trial.

For the first few days after the murders, Corazon Amurao was under sedation. The entire time, cops and prosecutors were still grilling her. They got very very lucky. Amurao wasn't intimidated by Speck and agreed to identify and testify against him.

The cops took Amurao up to Speck's hospital room and opened the door. He lay there on the bed, with tubes leading out of his body. Amurao stood at the doorway and looked in.

"That is the man," she told police.

Because of recent Supreme Court rulings, police were handling the case by the book. Cops didn't even attempt to question Speck without his lawyer present. Once identified and charged, Speck was assigned Cook County's chief public defender as his counsel. The public defender initially stated he would seek an insanity defense. That would change to a straight plea of "Not guilty." The penalty for conviction on any of the murder one charges was death in Illinois's electric chair.

It would take another year for pretrial motions. Everything was in readiness by April 1967 to try Speck for "the crime of the century." The star witness was scheduled to be Corazon Amurao. Public Defender Gerald Getty asked to have the trial moved to a different venue from Cook County, where pre-pretrial publicity had tainted the jury pool. The judge agreed and the trial was moved to Peoria, 150 miles from Chicago.

On April 5, 1967, the Filipino nurse Corazon Amurao, then barely one year in the U.S., entered the Peoria courthouse wearing a tailored cloth coat with white stitching outlining the sharply cut collar. The coat was probably as much protection against the cold weather as any fashion statement. She was accompanied by a beefy bailiff wearing a raincoat, shoulders hunched against the winter chill, who towered over the barely five-foot-tall, 100-pound woman.

The courtroom had fifty-eight spectators, including four fathers, two mothers, a brother, and a sister of the victims. Thirty others waited outside for a chance to get a seat in the stifling courtroom. The air-conditioning had failed but they didn't care. Amurao would be testifying in what till then was the most notorious mass murder in the United States. She had been extensively interviewed and debriefed by both Chicago detectives and attorneys, including the chief prosecutor, William Martin, from the State's Attorney's Office.

Martin did not take for granted that just because they had fingerprints tying Speck to the crime scene they would get a conviction. It all hinged on Amurao's thin shoulders. To boost his case, Martin made sure that Amurao referred to the defendant as "Speck" not "Mr. Speck" or "Richard Speck" or even "the defendant." Not giving him any dignity would serve to dehumanize Speck in front of the jury. It also did not go unnoticed that one of the definitions of the word "Speck" is "small, inconsequential."

Amurao wasn't allowed into the courtroom until the state of Illinois called her to the stand. But when they did, she made quite an impression. Head high, shoulders back, she walked in. She had shed the coat. She wore a yellow blouse, green skirt, and black tights that made her look more like a schoolgirl than a nurse. Martin knew that slight inconsistencies with her postevent physical recollections of Speck could be exploited by public defender Gerald Getty. He needed to spell it out for the jury on direct testimony.

A little drama never hurt.

"Do you see the man in this courtroom that you saw that night?" Martin asked.

Amurao stood up, walked across the courtroom until she was within a few feet of Speck at the defense table, pointed at his pockmarked face and declared, "This is the man," in perfect English.

Then Martin took her through the details of how Speck got into the apartment and what he did.

"Could you show the jury how he tied you up?"

Amurao got up, stepped down off the stand and into the well of the courtroom. What happened next was an odd sight, surreal and indelible to anyone there. The Filipino girl from the small town of San Luis "sat down on the asphalt tile floor of the modernistic walnut-paneled courtroom, pretending that her ankles were bound and that her hands were tied behind her. Then she twisted and turned over on her stomach and wriggled on the floor," reported the *NY Times*.

All that to get a conviction. And now it was the defense's turn. Getty was using what novelist Ross Thomas would describe as the "Other guy Overby" defense. Getty had contended in his opening statement that Amurao did not initially describe the guy as pockmarked, Speck's most noticeable physical feature, when she first spoke to the cops after the murders. Ergo, Corazon Amurao must be wrong now when she said Speck was the guy, when in fact it was the "other guy" whodunit.

"Does he look any different today than he looked that night in July?" Getty asked Amurao on cross examination.

"He's just the same," Amurao replied.

In his opening statement earlier, Getty had scored some points with the jury when he pointed out that the police artist who drew the sketch of the suspect based on Amurao's recollection drew a man with an unblemished face and crew cut, the direct opposite of Speck. Now he bore in on the foundation he had established earlier.

It was to officer Pomme, the cop who went to the basement and found nothing while Kelly proceeded through the brownstone and found everything, that Amurao had given her initial statement. On cross examination, Getty referred back to it.

"And was that description you gave to officer Pomme, 'a man twenty-five years of age, six feet tall, short crew cut hair, no hat, wearing a black waist-length jacket, dark pants?' " Getty asked.

"I did not say the crew cut, sir."

"You did not say crew cut?"

"No," said Amurao firmly.

"So if officer Pomme wrote that down, then he's incorrect?"

Translation: Under oath are you willing to call a Chicago cop a liar? In County Cemetery in Cleveland, Eliot Ness was smiling in his grave.

"I did not say that, sir," Amurao answered smoothly.

"You didn't say that?"

"I didn't say that."

"Now you never told officer Pomme that this man had marks on his face, did you?" Getty bore in.

"I told him he have marks on his face," Amurao answered.

"And if he didn't write it down, he should have, is that correct?"

"I don't know if he wrote it down."

That answer challenged Getty's assertion that

his client wasn't the guy because Amurao failed to mention he was pockmarked when first questioned by Pomme. In fact, she had mentioned it to Pomme.

"Did you tell officer Pomme that the man standing in the door was standing with a gun in one hand and a knife in the other?"

"No sir," Amurao answered firmly. "I just tell him that he have the gun in his right hand."

"So he would be wrong if he stated in a report that you told him the man had a gun in his right hand and a knife in the left hand?"

"I did not tell him that he had a knife in the other hand."

"Now the description that you gave the [sketch] artist on that day, can you recall what you told the artist?"

"I cannot recall, sir, what I tell him."

"No? So you can't recall whether you told the artist that he had marks on his face or not?"

"Yes. I can recall that I told him he had marks on his face, but all the other description I cannot recall. But also I emphasized to the artist about his hair."

"You emphasized about his hair?"

"Yes, I emphasized to the artist that it is the hair that was combed like that," and she mimicked the hairstyle with her hands, "going back, but he just draw it like that."

"But he showed you the finished product when he left?" using an American colloquial expression.

"Yes, but I told him that the hair is not like that."

"You told the artist the hair was not like that?"

"Yes," Amurao stated firmly.

"Yet he took it out of the room?"

"Yes, he just leave it like that."

"And put it in the police report?" Getty questioned.

"I don't know where he put it."

"You never told the artist he had a crew cut?"

"I did not tell him that."

That meant the sketch artist screwed up when he released a sketch of the suspect with a crew cut. Getty knew that he couldn't cross the line of appearing hostile to Amurao with all she had been through. The jury would hate him for that and convict Speck on a dime. Instead, the attorney walked that line skillfully while doing his job as Speck's advocate in challenging her testimony.

Getty put up two alibi witnesses who claimed Speck was drinking with them at the time of the murders. Their testimony was not convincing. In an apparent ploy to play on emotion, the defense also put up Speck's mother and six brothers, who testified to Speck's troubled background.

During his summation, prosecutor Martin detailed the injuries to the victims. "Speck had the strength in his hands and wrists and in the sinews of his arms to strangle the last breath from her innocent body . . . Speck had the strength to slit her throat six inches. Speck had the strength to stab her eighteen times . . . Speck had the strength to plunge a knife in her heart . . .

"But he did not have the strength to take his own life," the prosecutor concluded, which would have saved the state the cost of a trial and the electricity to execute him.

During his summation, defense attorney Getty contended that Speck was not the killer. He mentioned the alibi witnesses, and what he considered dubious fingerprint evidence linking his client to the crime scene. He claimed "a hasty judgment by higher-ups in the Chicago Police Department" led to Speck's arrest. Getty also continued to maintain that Amurao had initially given the police an incomplete characterization of Speck, which she had already denied convincingly on cross examination.

"If there's a reasonable doubt, it must come from your mind and conscience. You have the authority of kings," said Getty.

Very eloquent. Getty was a death penalty specialist. Going into the Speck trial he was 402 for 402. In 402 capital murder cases, not one of his clients had been executed in the electric chair.

Judge Herbert C. Paschen then charged the jury with the law and sent them out to deliberate. Forty-eight minutes later they were back. As Speck chewed on a piece of gum, the jury foreman, a steel and wire company foreman, delivered eight first degree murder convictions. Speck hardly seemed surprised, though he did fail to blow a bubble. The jury of seven men and five women recommended to the judge that he impose the death penalty. The judge, of course, could show mercy and simply incarcerate Speck.

He didn't.

On June 5, 1967, the judge sentenced Speck to die in Illinois's electric chair. Speck said nothing in his own defense, apparently content to sizzle. But someplace in the existential darkness of Richard Speck's soul, he got a break from an unlikely source.

Five years later, on June 29, 1972, the Warren Supreme Court effectively outlawed the death penalty in the United States. In a 5-4 vote, it struck down the death penalty statutes in forty states, including Illinois, calling the death penalty "cruel and unusual" punishment that violated the Eighth Amendment. Among the 629 inmates whose lives were spared and sentences commuted to life was Richard Speck.

In 1988, Speck was serving his time at Stateville State Prison when he decided to use a home video camera to make a little present for the state of Illinois. In the tape, Speck, sporting female breasts as the clear result of ingesting female hormones, has oral sex with fellow inmate Ronzelle Larimore. Larimore rubbed money on Speck's buttocks and forced the bills into his rectum.

Sitting in women's underwear, Speck tells Larimore, "If they only knew how much fun I was having, they would turn me loose." The tape would not surface until 1998, when someone finally smuggled it out of prison and sold it to a producer who went public with his "scoop."

On December 5, 1991, two days before his birthday, Richard Speck died of a heart attack at the age of forty-eight. With the liver of a hundred-year-old and a face that looked like it had melted, Speck had only served nineteen years behind bars when he dropped dead. Since nobody claimed his corpse, it became the problem of the state to dispose of his body. And it was a problem.

Anyone preparing Speck for burial would have noticed that he'd grown breasts. That would have meant delaying his burial for autopsy that would have disclosed the obvious—that Speck had grown breasts as the result of shooting up female hormones. How could he get female growth hormone in jail? In 1998 when the tape went public, it would be disclosed that guards had smuggled it in to him.

If Speck were buried, no matter the degree of decomposition that occurred, his remains would still contain evidence of the female growth hormone. At a future date if someone had suspicions, he could easily be dug up and tested. It was much easier to just destroy all the evidence. With everything to lose, Richard Speck's body was consigned to the retort, as the cremation chamber is called in the funeral trade. It was the only place he could have gone.

The container holding Speck's body—a cheap coffin the state uses when a prisoner dies—was placed in the retort. While laws vary from state to state, it is common for only one casket or container to be cremated at a time. It would be nice to think that some innocent's remains did not get mixed up with the mass murderer's.

The crematory operator raised the temperature dial to approximately 1600 to 1800 degrees. Soon, flames filled the retort around the coffin containing Speck's body. Over the next two to two and a half hours the coffin quickly burned up. Then the heat and flames went to work on the body. As it began burning down, the unmistakable stench of burning flesh—a smell so primal that all humans, regardless of their backgrounds, recognize it immediately—filled the air.

As Speck's flesh burned, and the flames quickly took care of that wretched tattoo—"Born to Raise Hell"—all of the liquid in his body evaporated. All of his skin, hair, fat, muscle, nails—they all vaporized. At the end of the two and a half hours of constant flame and heat, the only thing left was ash and small bone fragment, collectively referred to as "cremains," cremated remains.

The bone fragments and body metal—in Speck's case, numerous fillings—were swept to the back of the cremation chamber into a cooling pan made out of stainless steel. Through visual inspection and then the use of powerful magnets, the crematory operator separated the metal from the bone. The remaining bone fragments were then put into a grinder, where they were processed into coarse-grain sand that was whitish, light grainy gray. These particles of what once had been the physical essence of Richard Speck were placed in a cardboard receptacle provided by the crematorium.

His ashes were then taken by the state to an undisclosed location.

*O*nce the Speck case was successfully adjudicated, Corazon Amurao did not lose time in going on with her life.

On January 5, 1969, three years after the murders, at the age of twenty-five, she went back to the Philippines and got married. Her new husband, Alberto Atlenza, was a twenty-two-year-old law school graduate. At San Luis, her hometown fifty miles outside of Manila, a thousand mostly uninvited guests saw Amurao get married in an emotional thirty-five-minute ceremony. She held back the tears until the very end.

After the wedding, Amurao said that she and her husband Alberto planned to immigrate to the United States. She had not been deterred by her Chicago experience. If anything, it seemed to strengthen her resolve to try for her piece of the American dream.

Amurao told a UPI reporter, "We feel it would be a safer and nicer place to raise a family with as much of the important privacy we could have."

At the time, the dictator Ferdinand Marcos and his clotheshorse wife Imelda, who also had a shoe fetish, controlled the country with an iron fist. The couple did come back to the United States to live and raise their family. Given Amurao's green card status in the mid-1960s, and the fact that she stayed in the United States until at least 2000, she probably became a United States citizen. The Philippines would also allow her to maintain dual citizenship.

Part of that time she spent back to the Chicago area. I checked out the addresses I had for Corazon Amurao in the Chicago suburban towns of Melrose Park, Bartlett, and Lincolnwood. As expected, they were old ones. She was long gone.

Except for her comments to the UPI reporter when she got married, Amurao has granted no interviews since the murders, or at least none that I could find, and I looked hard. The same with her name. Finding someone with the name Corazon Amurao should be easy. It's an uncommon name, which means it will stand out in just about any database. But that assumes that the name has in some way been entered into a particular database.

When I attempted an outreach to an influential member of the Filipino community, I received an e-mail that said, "I do not know Corazon personally nor how to get in touch with her, unfortunately." I was beginning to get the feeling that Ms. Amurao not only didn't want to be found, she was making it her business not to be.

None of the nursing organizations I consulted had her in their databases, or so they told me. More likely, after all she has been through, they are respecting her wish to remain anonymous. Corazon Amurao does not want to be found. That is consistent with what she did that night and what she has done since. To the Filipino nursing community in the United States, she remains a legend, a quiet inspiration of the way to go about a decent life.

And then information surfaced on her through a strange source. The last thing anyone would have expected in 1966 was that the Speck case would inspire a play. Called *The Crime of the Century,* the play opened at the Circle Theater in Forest Park, Illinois, during the summer of 1999.

It took a closer look at the lives of the nurses and celebrated Amurao as a real heroine. The play also revealed that Corazon Amurao had become a critical care nurse in the Washington, D.C., area. She was performing that function as late as 1999 when she was living in northern Virginia. She was also a grandmother.

Paralleling Lake Michigan on the east as I drove north I now knew how Amurao had survived to become a grandmother and begat another two generations. It wasn't as simple as hiding and not being found. That was just part of it. Another piece was that Richard Speck was a functioning alcoholic in some ways, and in others was just plain dumb.

Speck was an idiot. He forgot how many nurses there were because two were added later. It was that fortuitous circumstance combined with Amurao's hiding that saved her life. So when Speck went into that room the last time and found it empty of nurses, Speck, a moron of the first order, had lost count. He was also tired. He had to be. Even for a lower order of human life like Richard Speck, the act of killing eight human beings manually rather than with an automatic weapon had to be physically tiring.

Any way you look at it, God was there. He had to be. Otherwise Corazon Amurao wouldn't be reading these words.

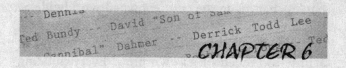
Survivor: Tracy Edwards
Serial Killer: Jeffrey Dahmer
aka "Milwaukee Cannibal"

*H*ow did Tracy Edwards get away? How did Tracy Edwards use his second chance at life that none of Jeffrey Dahmer's other sixteen victims had? To find those answers, I followed the concrete ribbon of highway. Interstate 94. I'd been on it since Chicago, happily leaving Richard Speck back there in the retort.

Heading north through the Wisconsin countryside, the highway went straight toward the horizon. It was bordered by snow-covered fields that stretched in an unbroken line for miles and miles. As the road took a rare uphill jog, at the top, in the distance, Milwaukee appeared out of the fields, her smokestacks belching gray smoke that stood out sharply against a cerulean blue sky.

Closer in, it became clear that many of those

smokestacks were attached to the brewing companies that made the city renowned worldwide as the beer capital of the United States. Milwaukee, though, looked old and worn-out, like it had drunk a little too much of its own brew. Every building in sight had a stately nineteenth century architectural elegance to it, covered over with a century's worth of soot. It was as if the place had frozen in time, during one of its colder winters, and never thawed.

Milwaukee had tried to change with the times. Asians, Hispanics, and blacks had made considerable inroads into what once was an all-white population. But like any inner city, it was still the people on the lowest end of the economic and social spectrum, the ones with little or no hope of moving up the ladder, who sometimes turned to criminal behavior to support themselves. In turn, police stereotyped minorities as lawbreakers and whites as the victims. To accept otherwise would be to challenge the natural order of the way things had always been.

It was a cold February day, the wind chill about ten below. I had been from one end of the country to the other. I was nearing the end of my journey. Wisconsin was a good place for answers. It is one of only thirteen states that do not have the death penalty. What that means is profound when studying any Wisconsin murder case.

Once the death penalty is taken off the table for even the vilest of crimes there is no drama except that of innocence or conviction. With mortality removed, it becomes much easier to examine the case and see patterns that would not be there if all the attention were focused on killing the criminal. Free of that emotional encumbrance, it becomes easier to see that the Dahmer case is all about race, the race of the killer and the race of the victims. To treat it any other way would be totally disingenuous.

Why race is not readily discussed when the case comes up is easy to understand. It's much easier to look at Jeffrey Dahmer in the one-dimensional way of making him the butt of jokes of some hack late night comic, instead of as a symbol of how lives can be lost when a police force allows itself to be blinded by the racism. It also serves as an object lesson on community policing, a popular term that in the 1950s meant that the neighborhood cop on the beat always knew what was happening and didn't look down on the people he was serving.

It was just before 2:00 A.M. when Lauren Davis called 911 to report the boy running around "butt naked." She didn't know who he was, but she knew he was terrified.

"One Adam 11, one Adam 11, see the woman. There's a boy running around butt naked."

The location followed. Police officer Jim Rhodes then jotted the information down in his notebook. His partner, Pete Melton, who was behind the wheel, tooled their squad car through the run-down streets of Milwaukee. When they got to their call, an argument was ensuing between two black women and a tall blond man. No, he didn't have one black shoe; he was wearing sneakers instead.

Then there was the Asian kid. He looked like he was *really* out of it, sort of drugged and shook up. He was sitting on the curb with a blanket over his shoulder. He looked up at the tall blond man arguing with the two black women.

The tall blond man told the cops that Konerak—that was the Asian boy's name—was his nineteen-year-old lover. Konerak drank too much, flipped out, and ran onto the street. The cops tried questioning Konerak but he was too "drunk" to make any sense. Had the cops given the boy his civil rights—that is, an interpreter—they would have figured out that the boy was from Laos, that he spoke Laotian, and that he was screaming in Laotian that the tall blond guy was about to kill and eat him. Now, while a Laotian interpreter may be hard to come by in downtown Milwaukee on a Saturday night at 2:00 A.M., you didn't need one to see that the kid was scared out of his wits.

Lauren Davis had been listening, and now she spoke up. She and her cousin had seen the half-naked boy trying to pull away from the tall blond man. He definitely was *not* his lover. But the cops seemed more interested in what the tall blond man had to say instead of the two black girls; they seemed so *strident*. Rhodes and Melton offered to escort Konerak back to the tall blond man's apartment. It was just a block away, and they got there within minutes.

Inside, the apartment smelled awful. It was a stench hard to define at first—hard to accept, more likely—but known to seasoned police officers. The cops found themselves in a living room off of which was the kitchen and a bedroom. Konerak's clothing was folded neatly on the sofa. On a coffee table, cops saw photographs of Konerak posing in black bikini briefs. As for Konerak himself, he sat down on the sofa and began muttering incoherently. His "lover" produced a photo ID that said he was "Jeffrey Dahmer." He kept reassuring the police that everything was all right.

Rhodes and Melton might have been wondering what was in the other rooms of the apartment, but that made no difference. They knew that without a search warrant issued by a court, anything they found in that room, or anyplace else in Dahmer's apartment, could not be used as evidence. Besides, what was there to find? The last thing cops anyplace want is to get in the middle of a lovers' quarrel.

Rhodes and Melton might also have run Dahmer's name through the computer in their squad car, which was connected to a mainframe at police headquarters. It was that same computer on which they regularly ran the names of people they stopped for traffic infractions. Had they given Dahmer the same respect as a traffic violator, a search would have disclosed that Jeffrey Dahmer was a convicted child molester on probation.

Rhodes and Melton preferred to take the word of a tall, blond, white man over two black girls and an Asian kid who couldn't talk, for whatever reason. Convinced that Dahmer was telling them the truth, they decided their work there was done. If Dahmer wanted to shack up with his nineteen-year-old lover, that was his business. After all, the boy was of age.

He wasn't, of course. Dahmer had lied. Konerak was actually fourteen years old. That made it statutory rape. But there were a lot of other things Rhodes and Melton didn't see. Like the three-day-old corpse laid out on Dahmer's bed, where he'd left it. Or the pieces of human flesh neatly arranged in his refrigerator, each with a different kind of meat tenderizer to make the experience that much more edible, that much more memorable.

By the time Rhodes and Melton got back in their squad car and drove off, Dahmer was in the process of strangling fourteen-year-old Laotian immigrant Konerak Sinthasomphone. That was his full name. Rhodes and Melton would have been grossed out by Dahmer's having sex with the body—in Milwaukee County, as in most places, a low level felony—dismembering it, and dining on Konerak for dinner.

Konerak Sinthasomphone was the thirteenth of Dahmer's seventeen victims. That's why I was on my way to Waukesha, Wisconsin. The one that got away lived there.

Jeffrey Dahmer was born in Milwaukee in 1960. As a tot, Jeffrey didn't seem any different from other kids. He loved the things most kids do, things like stuffed bunnies and wooden blocks. Physically, the boy had frequent ear and throat infections. It was during this time, someplace around the age of two, that Jeffrey and his father, Lionel, nursed an ill bird back to health and released it.

In 1962, Lionel moved the family to Iowa, where he was working on his Ph.D. at Iowa State. Two years later, when Jeff was four, he would later remember, his father swept out the remains of small animals underneath the house. The boy was thrilled by the sounds they made.

In 1966 the family moved again, to Doylestown, Ohio. That was a crucial year in the life of the Dahmer family. Jeff began first grade at Hazel Harvey Elementary School in Barberton, Ohio. When his brother David was born, Jeff's teacher reported that he felt neglected. Meanwhile, his parents were having problems and they moved into separate bedrooms. The year ended on a positive note when Jeffrey, suffering from a congenital double hernia, had surgery to correct the problem.

At age seven Jeff was starting to exhibit some of the classic signs of a budding serial killer. He made friends with a boy named Lee. He and Lee were real tight. Jeffrey had a teacher he liked a lot, and to show her how much, he gave her a bowl of tadpoles. The teacher then gave the tadpoles to his friend Lee.

Jeffrey killed the tadpoles with motor oil.

In 1968, during the year that both Martin Luther King Jr. and Robert F. Kennedy were assassinated, eight-year-old Jeffrey Dahmer began to show what Conan Doyle's Sherlock Holmes might describe "as a curious interest in the innards of animals." Jeffrey wanted to know how things worked right underneath the skin. Given a chemistry set as a present, he used it to experiment with animals. He impaled cats and frogs on sticks and preserved insects in jars.

One day while fishing, he caught a fish and reeled it in. Most kids would have taken it off the hook, either thrown it in a bucket to be eaten later or thrown it back in the sea. Not Jeffrey Dahmer. He chopped his into little pieces so he could see the inner workings.

In 1970, while most baby boomers were watching *The Mod Squad* on TV, ten-year-old Jeffrey was out collecting roadkill. He'd bleach chicken bones white, and indulge his love of insects by entombing them in jars filled with strange formaldehyde solutions. He decapitated small rodents, and after a bit of experimenting, learned how to use hydrochloric acid to strip meat off the bones of the roadkill.

Jeffrey was nothing if not precocious. In 1972, when he was twelve, as George McGovern was making his ill-fated run for the U.S. presidency, young Dahmer got his first job selling shrubbery. His boss was well-satisfied with his work, finding the pre-teen very "enthusiastic."

Writing in his 1994 memoir, *A Father's Story,* Lionel Dahmer says that only as Jeffrey grew older did he seem to withdraw within himself. Emotionally distant, with abandonment issues, Jeffrey liked to control people. It made up for his innate feelings of inadequacy. Lionel Dahmer, a chemist, speculates on the possibility that he passed on to his son a genetic predisposition to murder. He claims to have had murderous dreams, that Jeffrey as a failure reflected his own failings. He writes about Jeffrey's mother, who was depressed, who he claims took a lot of different kinds of pills during pregnancy, which may have influenced Jeffrey's genetics.

When he was thirteen, Jeff began drinking alcohol. This would become a life-long problem, much as it had been for Richard Speck. In 1974, he began attending Revere High School. Playing clarinet in the school band during freshman year, Dahmer later told investigators that he had his first homosexual experience that year, during which he began to regularly fantasize about having sex with a corpse.

The alcohol loosened him up a bit, so Jeff kept drinking, more heavily now. It helped the fifteen-year-old boy mature considerably. Dahmer now regularly carried plastic garbage bags; he was a collector of animal remains. He stripped the flesh from the bodies and mounted a dog's head on a stake.

The next year, classmates reported that Dahmer was drinking scotch regularly in class. They saw him as a desperate, lonely, immature boy. He did, however, attempt to join in by working on the school newspaper during his junior year. He played intramural tennis his sophomore through senior years. Dahmer was trying desperately to fit in.

During his senior year, Jeffrey Dahmer went to Washington, D.C., on a school trip. While there, he rang up the Vice President's office to chat with Walter Mondale. As for classroom work, he would trace the outline of bodies on the schoolroom floor with chalk.

For laughs.

The year 1978 was a major one for Jeffrey Dahmer. Having turned eighteen, he could now make decisions for himself. That was also the year his parents filed for divorce, his father moved out, and his parents had a custody battle over his twelve-year-old brother David. For Jeffrey, the stress was overwhelming. To cope with it, he had to kill. A human being. Time to stop experimenting on animals. He'd done that since childhood. He was an adult now, time to move on up the food chain.

Several days after his high school graduation, on June 18, 1978, Steven Hicks, eighteen years old, was picked up by eighteen-year-old Jeffrey

Dahmer. The former was a hitchhiker, the latter his ride. Dahmer invited Hicks back to his house. No one was home. They got drunk and had sex. Hicks tried to leave; Dahmer hit him in the back of the head with a barbell, killing him instantly. He dragged the body beneath the house then dismembered Hicks with a kitchen knife and placed the parts in plastic bags that he loaded in his father's car.

Feeling slightly better, Jeffrey watched as his parents legally divorced and his father won custody of his brother David.

Like so many serial killers before and after him when Dahmer set off for the town dump with the plastic bags, he made a mistake that attracted the police's attention. Cops stopped him after he drifted over the center line. He passed the field sobriety test. But the cops discovered the plastic bags. Why did they smell so bad?

Showing his cool, Dahmer set a pattern of remaining calm and being the best liar he could possibly be. He easily convinced the cops that the bags contained old, rotting, smelly garbage that he had forgotten for many days to take to the dump. The cops let the white boy go with a citation. Realizing his close call, Dahmer returned home to bury the bags in his backyard.

"That night in Ohio, that one impulsive night. Nothing's been normal since then," Dahmer later told the cops. "It taints your whole life. After it happened I thought that I'd just try to live as normally as possible and bury it, but things like that don't stay buried. I didn't think it would, but it does, it taints your whole life."

Then Dahmer showed the downhill swing common with serial killers. It is a series of bad breaks that leads to another type of break. In Dahmer's case, he tried to bury his past, to blot out his crime by enrolling at Ohio State University, where he majored in drinking prodigious amounts of alcohol. He also happened to get a little light-fingered, stealing a watch that didn't belong to him. Questioned about its disappearance, Dahmer dropped out to refine his drinking and other skills.

For a young man trying to find his place in society, a young murderer, what better place to soul-search than the anonymous United States Army? At the encouragement of Lionel's new wife Shari, Jeffrey Dahmer enlisted on December 29, 1978. He reported to Fort McClellan in Anniston, Alabama, hoping to become a military policeman.

Reassigned to Fort Sam Houston in San Antonio as a medical specialist, Dahmer was then sent to Baumholder, West Germany, to serve as a combat medic. While in Baumholder, there were five unsolved murders, involving mutilation. He drank heavily and got into Heavy Metal music, particularly Black Sabbath, and began a life-long interest in Satanism.

In March 1981, PFC Jeffrey Dahmer was discharged under an Army regulation concerning alcohol and drug abuse. It was not an honorable discharge, but rather, a general one. Returning home, he dug up the decomposing remains of Steven Hicks, little more than bones now. Pounding them with a hammer, he got rid of them in the forest.

Twenty-year-old Dahmer then moved to Miami Beach. He found work in a sandwich shop called Sunshine Subs. If you were in that shop from April through October 1981, Jeffrey Dahmer may have handled your food. By the end of the year he had driven up the turnpike to a Ramada Inn in Bath, Ohio. Dahmer got arrested there for disorderly conduct, having an open container, and resisting arrest. He subsequently moved to West Allis, Wisconsin, where he lived with his elderly grandmother.

In August 1982 he was arrested at the Wisconsin State Fair for drunk and disorderly conduct and fined fifty dollars. The following year, he got a job at the Milwaukee Blood Plasma Center. Taking home a vial of blood from work, he drank it and didn't like the taste. Jeffrey Dahmer was many things, but he was not a bloodsucker.

Unlike in George Orwell's novel, the year 1984 was a calm one in the budding serial killer's life. He got a job at the Ambrosia Chocolate Company, earning nine dollars an hour. He began attending church. He also hid in a department store, stole a male mannequin, took it home and had sex with it. His grandmother found it and threw it away.

In 1986, Dahmer was arrested for a third time when two boys accused him of masturbating in front of them in public on the banks of the Kinnickinnic River. Dahmer claimed he was urinating; he did not know the boys were there. The charges were plea-bargained down to disorderly conduct, one year probation.

In 1987, Dahmer was kicked out of a gay bathhouse, Club Baths. He was accused of drugging people in his private room at the club in order to have his way with them. That was the tip-off to what was to come. Dahmer was perfecting the part of his M.O. called "Method" by criminologists.

On September 15, 1987, Jeffrey Dahmer picked up Steven Toumi, a twenty-five-year-old white guy at a gay bar called Club 219. They left together to rent a room at the Ambassador Hotel. At the hotel, Dahmer passed Toumi a drink that contained the prescription drug Halcion. He drank it.

The *American Heritage Dictionary* defines "Mickey Finn" as a noun. It's slang for "an alcoholic beverage that is surreptitiously altered to induce diarrhea or stupefy, render unconscious, or otherwise incapacitate the person who drinks it. Probably after a notorious Chicago bar shut down in 1903, allegedly because its customers were served spiked drinks and then robbed."

When Dahmer doctored Toumi's drink with Halcion, he was just following in a long line of American murderers who drugged their victims with a "Mickey Finn" before killing them. Halcion is prescribed by physicians as a short-term medicinal treatment for insomnia. It puts you to sleep. A member of the powerful benzodiazepine class of drugs, many of the latter are used as tranquilizers. Leading up to unconsciousness, Halcion's side effects include coordination problems, dizziness, drowsiness, headache, light-headedness, nausea/vomiting, and nervousness. Dahmer figured it would be good to knock someone out with, and quickly.

The usual dosage for an adult is .25 milligrams, but never more than .5 milligrams. No telling how much Dahmer gave his victim. Dahmer claimed that he awoke the next morning to find him dead. Toumi had blood coming out of his mouth. Dahmer, though, stated he could not remember the previous night's events.

Like Raymond Burr in *Rear Window,* he bought a suitcase and put the corpse in it. He got a cab, put the bags inside, and returned with it to his grandmother's basement, where he masturbated on the corpse, had sex with it, and then sliced the flesh off it. Dismembering the body, he put the pieces into plastic bags and threw them away. Toumi was subsequently reported missing.

"After that, it all started again," he later said.

Club 219 seemed to be good luck for Dahmer. He frequented the place more and more. In January 1988, Dahmer picked up fourteen-year-old male prostitute, James Doxtator, outside the club. Invited to accompany Dahmer back to his grandmother's house, where he could earn money posing nude, Doxtator willingly went to the tall blond guy's place, where they had sex.

Dahmer put some sleeping pills into the boy's

drink, waited till he had a good long draught and passed out, and then had his way with him. He strangled Doxtator and then dismembered the corpse with a knife. A sledgehammer helped him break the bigger bones while acid helped to strip down the flesh. When James Doxtator's body had finally been dismantled, Dahmer threw the remains in the garbage.

Three months later, on March 24, Dahmer was at a bar called the Phoenix when he met up with an available guy, twenty-five-year-old Richard Guerrero. Using the old "I'm gonna make a porn video with you" trick, he lured Guerrero back to his grandmother's house. They had oral sex together. When Guerrero got thirsty, Dahmer mixed him one of his Mickey Finns. It knocked him out, whereupon Dahmer fell upon Guerrero and strangled him to death. Adding up the felonies, Dahmer had sex with the corpse. Once satiated that way, he dismembered what had once been a human being and threw it away like so much detritus.

In September 1988, Dahmer's grandmother Catherine finally asked him to move out. What with his strange hours and the stink from his experiments, it was just too much to take. On September 25 Dahmer moved into an apartment in an old run-down section of Milwaukee on North 24th. He met Somsack Sinthasomphone the next day.

Dahmer smooth-talked the thirteen-year-old Laotian boy into coming back to his apartment to pose for nude pictures for fifty dollars. Once there,

Dahmer gave him the Mickey Finn—Irish cream liqueur and crushed Halcion tabs. The kid got partially undressed and Dahmer took two Polaroids. While the kid was dopey, Dahmer touched the boy's penis and kissed his stomach. But he didn't fall unconscious, which saved his life.

Dahmer was too much of a coward to kill anyone who might resist. He let the boy go. When he got home, his parents took him to the hospital. But this time Dahmer's luck ran out. The kid gave the cops a description, and they eventually tracked Dahmer down to the Ambrosia Chocolate Company, where he still worked.

Charged with exploitation of a child and second degree sexual assault, Dahmer pleaded not guilty at his preliminary hearing and was freed on $2,500 cash bail. Trial was set for May 1989. Dahmer, though, gave it some thought, and on January 30, 1989, changed his plea to guilty. He was allowed to remain free on bail pending sentencing.

Three months later, on March 29, Dahmer went to a new gay bar, La Cage Aux Folles, where he met a twenty-four-year-old black man, Anthony Sears. Using what had now become his practiced M.O., Dahmer lured Sears back to his grandmother's house—he figured the cops were staking out his apartment—to be photographed for money. Once there, they had sex, and sex of course brings on an incredible thirst. Time for the old Mickey Finn, which put Sears straight out.

Dahmer jumped on his limp body and strangled

him. As was now usual, he had sex with the corpse
and dismembered the body. He threw a new wrinkle
in when he decided to act on his impulse of taking
the victim's decapitated head and boiling it. Then,
"I took the knife and took the scalp part off and
peeled the flesh off the bone and kept the skull and
the scalp. If I could have kept him longer, all of him,
I would have." Dahmer completed the job by paint-
ing the skull gray. He kept it as a souvenir of a job
well done. But it was the last killing for a while.

On May 23, 1989, Dahmer was finally found
guilty of second degree sexual assault and enticing
a child for immoral purposes in the case of Somsack Sinthasomphone. The judge sentenced him to
eight years of hard time. The sentence was commuted to one year. Later that year, he was given
a twelve-hour pass to go home for Thanksgiving.
He used the privilege to go to a bar and get drunk
instead of going home for Thanksgiving dinner.

When he woke up the next day, a man was sexually assaulting him with a candlestick. Dahmer was
all tied up. He got back from his prison furlough
late. Tired and frustrated with prison life, he wrote
a letter to the prison board petitioning for leniency.
He was persuasive. The board listened and gave
him parole on December 10, 1989. Dahmer had
only served ten months. As part of his parole, he
was ordered to stay away from minors.

When Jeffrey was convicted of child molesta-
tion in 1989, his father realized that his son would
"never be more than a liar, an alcoholic, a thief, an

exhibitionist, a molester of children . . . I could not imagine how he had become such a ruined soul. For the first time I no longer believed that my efforts and resources alone would be enough to save my son. There was something missing in Jeff. We call it a 'conscience.' That had either died or had never been alive in the first place."

Upon his release from prison, Dahmer rented Apartment 213 at the Oxford Apartments on Milwaukee's North 25th Street. It was a forty-nine-unit low-rise building in a crime-infested neighborhood. Dahmer's neighbors soon noticed and complained about a bad smell emanating from his apartment that they couldn't quite define. He also had a predilection for using a noise-polluting power saw at odd hours of the night. Dahmer claimed that he had a few woodworking projects going and that he was building bookcases.

In June 1990, down at the Phoenix bar, Dahmer made the acquaintance of twenty-eight-year-old Edward Smith. Dahmer was more direct this time, suggesting to Smith that they go back to his place to have sex. Smith agreed. They made love in Dahmer's apartment, and then Dahmer in his black widow mode fed Smith the Mickey Finn. After his collapse, Dahmer strangled him.

Just weeks later, in July, Dahmer was at his old haunt the Club 219, where he met Raymond Smith, aka "Ricky Lee Beeks." After luring him back to his place, Dahmer made him his seventh victim. He engaged in necrophilia, and then used Soilex to take the flesh off the bones, making them easier to dispose of as little trinkets placed around his apartment. He kept Smith's skull in his refrigerator as a sort of souvenir of the experience.

The killings were escalating in frequency. On September 2, 1990, twenty-four-year-old Ernest Miller was offered fifty dollars by Dahmer to pose nude. They had intercourse at Dahmer's apartment. After Dahmer drugged him into unconsciousness, he did what serial killers sometimes do: he changed his M.O. Instead of strangling Miller, he neatly cut his throat, killing him in a pool of his own blood.

Dahmer was hungry. He cut out Miller's biceps and put them in the freezer. They'd make a tasty snack later. Come to think of it, why not keep the entire skeleton? He used one of his acidic compounds to deflesh Miller's bones. Cops would later find the skeleton in Dahmer's apartment. When they questioned him about it, Dahmer confessed:

> I separated the joints, the arm joints, the leg joints, and had to do two boilings. I think I used four boxes of Soilex for each one, put in the upper portion of the body and boiled that for about two hours and then the lower portion for another two hours. The Soilex removes all the flesh, turns it into a jelly-like substance and it just rinses off. Then I laid the clean bones in a light bleach solution, left them there for a day and spread them out on

either newspaper or cloth and let them dry for
about a week in the bedroom.

Three weeks later, twenty-two-year-old David
Thomas met thirty-year-old Jeffrey Dahmer. Ever
the gentleman, Dahmer invited him back to his
apartment for drinks. Enter Mickey Finn. But once
again Dahmer changed his M.O. He dismembered
David Thomas while he was alive, but too drugged
and unconscious—hopefully—to do anything
about it.

While Dahmer was in the process of using the
implements of his death trade, he took Polaroids of
the actual dismemberment. In this instance, there
were some rare poses of Thomas's severed head,
placed in various locations throughout the apartment. Thomas's sister would later view these shots
in order to make a positive identification.

On March 7, 1991, Dahmer picked up eighteen-
year-old Curtis Straughter. He suggested that
Straughter pose for pictures, and they went back
to Dahmer's flat. Dahmer changed his M.O. again.
He was getting bolder now and beginning to take
chances. While Straughter was performing oral sex
on him, Dahmer strangled him with a leather strap.
Had Straughter been stronger and fought back,
there might have been a different outcome. Hungry once again, and forever the souvenir hunter,
Dahmer kept Straughter's genitals, hands, and, of
course, his skull.

He had quite a collection by now.

One month later, on April 7, Dahmer met Errol Lindsey, nineteen, at a bus stop near a bookstore that featured gay issues. Inviting the young man back to his apartment, Dahmer went back to his old M.O., drugging the boy and strangling him. He then added a new wrinkle to his necrophilia tendencies by having oral sex with the corpse. He kept his skull for his growing collection.

Showing that he was an equal opportunity serial killer, Dahmer next picked up thirty-one-year-old Tony Hughes, who was deaf, at Club 219. Dahmer passed Hughes a note at the bar with a proposition to come back to his apartment to pose nude for fifty dollars. Hughes wrote down "Sure," and he accompanied Dahmer back to his apartment. Dahmer drugged and strangled Hughes, but for some reason he didn't dispose of his corpse immediately. He left it on his bed, to swell up and putrefy in the intense summer heat.

Mistakes. Dahmer was making mistakes. Strangling someone alive who could fight back, leaving a corpse on his bed to decompose, to bring him attention. He was nearing the end and all but asking to be found out. With Konerak Sinthasomphone on May 27, 1991, he almost met his serial killer Waterloo. It turned out, by coincidence, that Konerak was the brother of Somsack Sinthasomphone, the boy Dahmer had sexually assaulted in 1988.

But even the murder of teenage prostitutes and black men eventually gets the attention of the public, as it did during the sweltering summer of 1991.

The city's police finally became aware that twelve people were missing and presumed dead. Rumors on the street said it was a white man preying on blacks. Racial tensions accelerated toward who knew what?

That "what" turned out to be more killings.

On June 30, 1991, Jeffrey Dahmer met twenty-year-old Matt Turner at a bus station in Chicago after the Gay Pride Parade. Sharing a Greyhound bus together back to Milwaukee, they hit it off and Dahmer invited Turner back to his apartment, where he drugged and strangled Turner. Dahmer kept Turner's head and organs in the freezer. Showing real creativity, Dahmer put the disembodied torso in a fifty-seven-gallon barrel of hydrochloric acid in his bedroom. The smell must have been dreadful, but the neighbors were already used to it.

Once again Jeffrey Dahmer, equal opportunity serial killer, came to the fore. His next victim was Jeremiah Weinberger, a Jewish twenty-three-year-old. Weinberger made Dahmer's acquaintance at a Chicago gay bar. Riding back to Milwaukee together on the Greyhound, Dahmer invited him back to his apartment, where they had sex. But Dahmer didn't kill him, at least not immediately. Weinberger got to spend the night in the serial killer's apartment.

In the morning, Weinberger wanted to leave. That just didn't sit well with Jeffrey, who offered him a drink. Once Weinberger was drugged and unconscious, Dahmer injected boiling water into his brain. Dahmer must have seen too many Ed Wood movies. He had some strange idea of creating a zombie love slave who would do his bidding. Weinberger lasted two days until he died from the hot water treatments. Dahmer later told cops:

"I came back from work the second night. He had died and it kind of struck me as particularly horrifying, because he was the only one that died with his eyes . . . his eyes were just wide open."

Dahmer dismembered Weinberger, put his head in the freezer and the torso in his ever-present barrel of acid. He followed up with victim number fifteen, twenty-three-year-old Oliver Lacy. When he met Lacy on the street, Dahmer had just been fired from his job at Ambrosia Chocolate. He invited Lacy back to his apartment. They made love and Dahmer did what had become the usual sexual behavior for him—drugging, murdering, and dismembering.

Lacy's head joined the others in the freezer collection, but Dahmer also had a new notion—he'd cut the guy's heart out and preserve the tasty morsel in the freezer too. But he was a bit hungry, so he cut out Lacy's bicep, used some meat tenderizer on it, and ate it. And since he was getting good at bleaching bones, he stripped all the gristle off the skeleton and kept it as the second in his valued collection.

Joseph Bradehoft, twenty-five, met Dahmer on July 19, 1991, at a bus stop. The brazen serial killer offered him money to come back to his place to pose nude for some Polaroids. Back at Dahmer's apartment, they had sex, after which Dahmer drugged Bradehoft and strangled him with a leather strap. He kept the corpse on his bed for two days before dismembering it and putting the torso in the acid barrel, the head in the freezer with the rest.

And then, on July 24, 1991, Jeffrey Dahmer met his match.

*T*racy Edwards and his twin brother Terrence were born on June 3, 1969. According to police records, Tracy Edwards has his brother's name, Terrence Edwards, as his "aka."

Tracy has a smiling, open face in his mug shot. He's five-eight and weighs 145 soaking wet, has wavy black hair and soulful brown eyes. It's easy to see why Dahmer would think he could get the better of him. What the serial killer missed in his analysis was a hardened determination behind those eyes and prominent cheekbones.

Edwards was twenty-two when he made the acquaintance of Dahmer, only nine years his senior. He's straight. Exactly how he fell for Dahmer's M.O. is hard to say. What is known is that Dahmer managed to lure him back to his apartment for drinks. He slipped Edwards the Mickey Finn, only this time, it didn't put the proposed victim out. The only way that could happen is simple—Dahmer miscalculated the amount of

Halcion, or whatever other doping drug he was using at the time.

With Edwards groggy but still fully conscious, Dahmer slapped a handcuff around his wrist. Dahmer made him watch some sort of porn video while threatening him with a knife. At that moment the internal mechanism that every human being has—and maybe some more so than others—to fight when death is imminent, found its way into the lightweight's fist.

What is fascinating is that in all the crimes to come on Tracy Edwards's record, nothing indicated he had Marvin Hagler's right. The fist found its target, someplace on Dahmer's head. The punch stunned the bigger man long enough to let Edwards run out through the apartment door and down to the street. In shades of the Konerak incident a few weeks before, a cruising squad car spotted Tracy running through the street with his still handcuffed wrist. While they knew he definitely wasn't "Richard Kimble," this time they listened as Tracy spun a strange tale about the "weird dude" who drugged him, made him watch some porn video, and threatened him with a knife.

This time, the cops listened to the African American. Accompanied by Tracy as guide, the cops went back to Dahmer's apartment. Dahmer opened his door at the sound of the sharp knocks. One more time, and this time for all the money—ugh, chocolate, ugh, whatever—Dahmer tried to bluff his way out of the situation. He claimed to have been so down over losing his job at the chocolate factory—it always helps to add a little truth to your lies—that he'd gotten drunk and lost his temper.

So he'd put some cuffs on his friend? Dahmer offered to get the key from his bedroom. Before hearing yes or no, he turned and went toward his bedroom. Again the cop did the right thing. Not knowing what Dahmer could be getting, a key or a gun, he followed him closely, and soundlessly. If Rod Serling were standing in the corner smoking a butt, intoning, "You are about to enter the Twilight Zone," things couldn't have gotten any weirder.

The cop spied dozens of Polaroids of dismembered bodies scattered about the bedroom. Walking into the kitchen, the cop noticed that the same refrigerator was in the background of the Polaroids. He opened the refrigerator door. Even though he was an experienced officer, he screamed at what he saw.

"There's a goddamn head in here!" he shrieked at his partner.

There was more than that. He hadn't gotten to the freezer . . . yet.

Suddenly, Dahmer dropped the calm demeanor his sociopathic personality had accumulated for the world at large. He was what he really was, a struggling, squealing, wild animal trying to escape from, literally, the arms of the law. The two cops finally got the better of him and handcuffed the cannibal. They took Dahmer down to police headquarters to be questioned by homicide detectives.

Tracy Edwards had seen the whole thing. Dahmer had threatened to "cut out your heart and eat it." He realized that the threat had been literal, had he not managed a Hagler right. Edwards was taken away by cops to get his statement, while detectives and forensic techies entered apartment 213 at Oxford Apartments on North 25th Street.

When they cracked the freezer, they found Dahmer's souvenirs—three human heads. He also had some other interesting "goodies." There were what looked like piles of human meat and two pair of hands. Searching further in a kitchen closet, detectives found a human penis in a stockpot, but no recipe.

On a shelf in the bedroom closet, detectives found two skulls that had been expertly defleshed. They were painted a nice shade of gray. They also found male genitalia preserved in formaldehyde. Cops discovered a bottle of chloroform. That indicated the drug was just his latest to use on unsuspecting victims. Rounding out the grisly discoveries were hundreds of photographs of the victims, both before and after being murdered.

Oh, yes, the cops also found the barrel of acids and inside, dissolving human remains.

On July 25, 1991, Jeffrey Dahmer was charged with four counts of homicide. He gave police a detailed confession. Knowing they had a stone-cold serial killer in custody, the Wisconsin court set bail at $1 million.

Dahmer eventually pleaded guilty but insane.

After a brief trial, during which an eighteen-feet-high barrier was erected to protect Dahmer from the very real threats of his victims' anguished families, he was convicted on February 5, 1992, on fifteen counts of homicide and sentenced to fifteen life terms, or 957 years behind bars.

To an eleven-year-old growing up near Milwaukee, the Dahmer case provided some interesting memories.

"The Dahmer fiasco happened just about the time I was becoming vaguely aware of current events," says Martin Kane, now an editor at a book publishing house. "I remember a lot of jokes about Ambrosia Chocolate—i.e., are there body parts in it?—and a lot of adolescent jokes about eating genitals and such.

"But what I do distinctly remember is the racial element and the police officers' trial. There was definitely some palpable tension over the officers' basically bigoted response to the earlier Dahmer incidents—the fact that they basically handed victims back to him because they were minorities, and because they thought, 'Oh, that's just what gays do . . . get naked and run around town covered in blood.'

"And then of course there was sympathy for the officers, because they were patrolling the ghetto and had to deal with crazy stuff like this every day, so how were they supposed to know this guy was a cannibalistic serial killer, etc.? Those were the two sides of the argument . . . and there was certainly a little O.J.-esque feeling to the proceedings, but it never reached that level, of course.

"The next thing I remember is when Dahmer was murdered in prison much later, along with another infamous Milwaukee convict who killed his wife in a ghetto parking lot and then said that it was a 'black youth' that did it . . . there was of course a lot of controversy around that situation as well."

On November 28, 1994, while on a work detail with another convict in a bathroom, African American Christopher Scarver sexually assaulted Dahmer and then beat him to death.

"After that, Milwaukee tried to forget about what happened," says Kane. "Every five years or so, there's a story in one of the local papers recapping the case. It always goes national."

The lurid details of the Dahmer case effected people across the country, and especially those in close proximity to the crimes. And Tracy Edwards, what did he do with his second chance?

I shivered in the Wisconsin cold and sprinted for the front double glass doors of the Waukesha County Sheriff's Department. Here, Tracy Edwards is well known.

"He's the one who got away," said the clerk who handed me a copy of his mug shot. "That's what he tells everyone. He loves to talk to the jailers. Every time he comes in here, he tells them how he got away."

Often, convicted criminals—even low-level ones like Edwards—do not have regular addresses. I lost track of how many addresses Edwards had in both Waukesha and Milwaukee. He was long gone from all of them. But his record did follow him.

On June 11, 1997, Tracy Edwards did a very foolish thing. He filed for bankruptcy with total debts of $8,865 and total assets of $2,241. What made it foolish was that for $6,624, he destroyed his credit for the next seven years. But in Tracy Edwards's milieu, destroying credit where none probably existed anyway, in order to pay off debts, was a good deal.

The next time Tracy Edwards's name hit the news was on April 9, 1998, when the *Milwaukee Journal-Sentinel* headlined a story:

**MAN WHO FLED DAHMER
JAILED IN DRUG CASE**

It seemed that Tracy had, once again, gotten himself into trouble. He was jailed in a drug paraphernalia case. The cops were also investigating whether Edwards and his two children had taken up residence with a Waukesha woman who then failed to report his presence in her home when filing for food stamps.

March 30, 2000, Tracy Edwards lost another one. This time it was the *State of Wisconsin, County of Waukesha* v. *Tracy M. Edwards*. Tracy had skipped out on his bail. The Wisconsin circuit court found for the plaintiff, the state, which meant the bail, $10,050, was forfeited. Whoever the bail bondsman was, it had not been a good deal.

In a "where are they now" article in the *Waukesha Freeman,* published July 23, 2001, the paper reported, "Edwards has been wanted for more than 22 crimes in Waukesha County alone . . ."

On March 7, 2002, Edwards was in trouble again, pleading "guilty" to "Bail-Jumping Felony." Then he moved back into Milwaukee County, where on April 19, 2004, cops busted him for "Possession of Cocaine," a misdemeanor. He pleaded guilty on May 19, 2004.

You know the expression a record as long as your arm? One of Edwards's lawyers whom I spoke with tried to get me to see that it is almost impossible to grow up black in Milwaukee without having to deal with an inherently racist system that often turns innocent people to crime because they have no hope in anything else.

I knew he was right. But Tracy Edwards was the *only* survivor of Jeffrey Dahmer. Didn't that come with a responsibility? It bothered me.

In Steven Spielberg's *Saving Private Ryan,* the entire film after D-Day is about this one platoon saving this one lowly grunt whose four brothers have all been killed. By presidential order, he gets a free pass. It was based on a real life case involving the five Sullivan brothers, who were all killed during World War II while serving on the same ship.

At the end of the film, Ryan is saved, but at what

price? The entire platoon, save one, has been killed in battle. As their captain, Tom Hanks, lies dying, the victim of a German sharpshooter, he pulls Private Ryan (Matt Damon) close and whispers, "Earn it!"

As I drove out of Waukesha, the computer flashed a warning on the dashboard, "Coolant needed." I bought some antifreeze at a crossroads convenience store. As I was pouring it into the coolant receptacle under the hood, I looked up at the traffic going by, kicking up ice and belching steam from hot tailpipes.

A car filled with kids went by. Their father was driving. I knew that someplace out here Tracy Edwards was still riding around. That was good; he had kids who needed him.

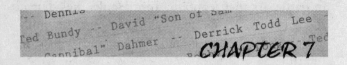

CHAPTER 7

Survivor: Carl Denaro
Serial Killer: David Berkowitz aka "Son of Sam"

Old Mother Hubbard/ Sitting near the cub bard
[sic]/ with a hand grenade under the oatmeal./
Who will you kill now/Daughter of Satan?/ In the
image of the/ Virgin Mary—pure and innocent/
The Great Impersonator—/ Is that you? "Yes."/
How many have you deceived—[sic]/ lured to
slaughter like a/ fat cow? (Abraham's 87)
—David Berkowitz

Back home in New York, the worn Grand Central Parkway took me into the heart of what locals call "the Island," and a town called Bellerose. Walking smoothly across the wet street, under a gray Long Island sky, Carl Denaro's smile is warm but wary, his handshake hard.

Denaro looks like a middle-age linebacker with a paunch, steel gray hair, sharp features, and light complexion. He had on glasses, looking younger than his forty-nine years. He wore a blue Polo jacket, collared blue shirt, and Gap trousers. The pub he had picked for lunch wasn't open yet, so we tooled around in his Jaguar for a while, killing time till it opened.

Stopping for some coffee, Denaro sat at a table in front of a high plate-glass window. He would later tell me that he never heard the sound of the glass shattering when he was shot by the Son of Sam. By noon, the pub Denaro had in mind had opened and we were transferred to a back booth that he preferred.

Sitting in the dark wood-paneled dining room, the left side of his face was lit by an overhead faux gas lamp, giving his New York pallor a yellowish tinge. He seemed comfortable there in the shadows, preferring to wake late and sleep late. Periodically, he exited to light up a cigarette. That he has a family makes no difference. Carl Denaro lives in some sort of existential place where none of it really matters.

"How could it, if you are supposed to be dead?" he asked. The metal plate deep in the back of his head is testament to the body's resiliency to heal itself. How far back in the psyche the bullet wound goes, though, is hard at first to determine.

"You know, none of Berkowitz's victims talk. The ones that survived, I'm the only one," he stated matter-of-factly, in sort of a gravelly voice.

Denaro is right. Many of Berkowitz's survivors had been maimed for life and did not want to talk about it. For Denaro, his survival is all about his background.

"My parents met at the upstate New York town of Otisville. I think my father was eight or ten when he got shipped off to an orphanage after his mother died. His father was left with ten kids to take care of, and he couldn't do it for all of them. Five were bringing in money; they stayed. My dad was one of the five who weren't. They went. He spent three years in the orphanage until he developed tuberculosis and was sent to a sanitarium in Otisville."

In the mid–twentieth century, Americans sought out drier climates to deal with the lung-debilitating effects of tuberculosis. Otisville, located at the foot of the Catskill Mountains, was an area of dry, clean air and moderate climate. It was here that Frank Denaro, patient, met and fell in love with a nurse. They married and had six kids.

"The middle three were more independent. I was one of them. I grew up not believing I needed someone's approval," he told me, let alone that of his parents. By the time Carl was a teenager, he was on his own and independent.

"I had long hair, very long hair. I just had it cut, probably about six or eight inches, because I was going in the Air Force in five days. October 28 was my report date. It was like a shag haircut. I didn't want to show up in basic training with really long hair, but looking back, I was a moron. It was still long."

He would be leaving his work as a security guard and part-time community college student behind, to serve his country. Denaro also had an active social life, which included clubbing and dancing. It was on such a night of social activity that he made the acquaintance of the soon-to-be legendary Son of Sam.

Serial killing was an almost unheard of crime in the twentieth century until the Son of Sam showed up in New York City in 1976. Not since Jack the Ripper in England a century earlier did a serial killer court headlines the way this guy did, and for good reason.

Not since the Ripper had a killer corresponded with the cops in quite so eloquent ways. Showing Saucy Jack's flare for the dramatic, Son of Sam even wrote a tabloid reporter directly, knowing it would gain him even greater fame. For a change, the killer's ego was warranted. The reporter's is another story.

From the summer of 1976 to the summer of 1977, the killer the tabloids first coined the ".44 Caliber Killer," and then later the self-described "Son of Sam," terrorized New Yorkers with a seemingly supernatural ability to appear at random, shoot down men and women in their prime, then melt away into New York City's streets. No one knew where Son of Sam was; no one knew when he would strike next. The guy was a maniac who always went for couples necking in cars.

In the fall of 1976, when the case started, there was no concept of what was to come, as with all serial killer cases. How could there be? Murders in New York City were commonplace and rampant, and in the 1970s in the city, lawlessness reined. Into this anarchic atmosphere, where criminals controlled the streets instead of the cops, came a killer unlike any they had ever seen before.

Clever, enterprising, he was smarter than they were, and he would not stop until caught.

July 29, 1976

Donna Lauria, eighteen, and her girlfriend Jody Valenti, twenty, sat in the car chatting. Lots of people did that in New York City. No one ever thought twice about it. Talking, necking, whatever, you were safe in your car. Or so it was assumed.

Lauria had parked the car in front of a prewar six-story apartment building in the Westchester Heights section of the Bronx where she lived with her parents. An emergency medical technician at Empire State Hospital, she and her friend Valenti, a nurse, were discussing plans for a late summer vacation.

A few moments later, Lauria's parents returned home from a night out, waved hello, said "Good night" to the girls, and entered the building, leaving Lauria and Valenti alone with their plans. That's when the guy seemed to come out of no place. First he wasn't there, and then he was.

Valenti saw him walk deliberately toward the driver's side of the car. Bringing up a long-barreled pistol, for a brief moment the man looked at them, and then came the explosions that never seemed to end. Valenti felt something in her left leg and looked down to see a bullet hole blossoming red. Lauria, though, was not so lucky. Hit in the back with what police later said was a bullet from a large caliber weapon, she died instantly.

Suspecting nothing out of the ordinary, and aware of no viable suspect, the NYPD detective on the case, Ronald Ascension told the press, "We have nothing," and then appealed to the public to help. Police set up a special phone number for tips on the case.

October 23, 1976

When the next assault occurred, it was not immediately attributed by police to the same shooter as the Lauria homicide. Perhaps that was because this time the shooter wasn't quite as successful.

"Carl Denaro, 20, a security guard at Citibank, was shot in the back of the head about 2:00 A.M. on Oct. 23, 1976, a Saturday, as he sat in a parked car with his girlfriend Rosemary Keenan, on 160th Street between 32nd and 33rd Avenues in Flushing, Queens," the *New York Times* reported dispassionately. Denaro's memories are much more specific.

"The weather, it was a warm night. I was wearing sneakers, Pumas. I liked the blue suede ones.

Or maybe my Chuck Taylors. I had on jeans and a flannel shirt. Construction boots."

It was a definite mid-1970s late teenage outfit.

"So I'm sitting in the passenger seat. It was Rosemary's car, a blue Volkswagen Beetle. Rosemary was a friend of mine from Queens Borough Junior College. She was chasing me around. She had brown short hair. We met up at Peck's in Flushing, on 166th Street and Crocheron Avenue. I went there often enough. We were there drinking at the bar. She wanted to be my girlfriend."

Sometime between 12:30 to 12:45 P.M. Denaro decided to end the chase. "I said, 'Let's go,' and we left. So we got in her car and drove down 149th Street and 35th Avenue in north Flushing. We didn't have a make-out place. This was my neighborhood. This is where I live. I lived on 149th Street and 35th Avenue. We were just looking for a dark street."

They were in St. Andrew's parish, at the time the richest parish in the New York archdiocese.

"There are a lot of rich people. There were well-kept English Tudors, whitewashed center hall colonials. All the houses were four, five, and six bedrooms, not quite mansions, but not too far away from them.

"So anyway, we just drove around, looking for a quiet, secluded, dark place." Inside the car, the windows were closed, their pores opening up with sweat and alcohol. "We wind up, and this is funny," he laughed, "I think it's funny, we wind up on 33rd Avenue and 159th Street. Your notes probably say 160th Street."

"No, they don't," I said. "I'm from Brooklyn—159th, 160th Streets, makes no difference, I'm still lost," and we both laughed.

"We're going down 159th Street. Now, five of my friends live on 159th Street. I'm still friends with three of them. At the end of 159th Street and 33rd there's a stop sign."

Just then Denaro saw a car going west on 33rd Avenue. Inside that car was the killer who called himself Son of Sam. Berkowitz had been out driving every night since July 1976, looking for a sign to kill. The situation would have to be perfect. If he could find a parking place for his car right away, if he could find some likely victims, he took that as a sign. When he got "the Calling," Berkowitz went looking for his victims.

"Then," Denaro continued, "Rosemary drove across the intersection. I said, 'Pull over here.' There were no streetlights. By the time she rolled to a stop, we were about thirty-five feet from the corner. There's a stick shift between us, the windows were closed, and it's dark."

Like kids from coast to coast, Denaro liked to have a little something with him on a date. In his case, it was a half pint of Jack Daniel's.

"I had a bottle of Jack Daniel's between my legs. It was two o'clock in the morning. I was pretty well looped. I unscrewed the cap, took a swig. We both leaned over and started kissing, groping. Next thing you know, there's glass all over the place.

"Now, for some reason I still can't remember why I did this, for some reason I had someone buy me two ounces of pot even though I was going in the Air Force in five days. And I had it on me. I didn't smoke that much. I obviously couldn't take it with me. Weird, anyway, the glass was shattering and I said, 'Get out of here.' I remember saying that. And then I passed out.

"When I woke up, we were at the corner of 33rd Avenue and 159th Street. Rosemary's in a tizzy. She's panicking. Now Rosemary's from Flushing and she doesn't know where we are, but I do. I woke up, looked around, and knew where we were. I directed her back to Peck's, which was just a series of rights. She pulled in front of Peck's. I had blood all over my hands. There's glass all over and I thought the car had exploded. Now at the time, Peck's was kind of a hoppin' place and they had three bartenders and a guy checking proof at the door. I knew all these guys."

Denaro slowly got out of the car, unaware of the blood coming from the bullet wound in the back of his head.

"So the guy at the door, he takes a look at me and he's like, 'What the hell happened to *you?*'

" 'The car blew up,' I said, and he says, 'You better sit down. You're white as a ghost.' So I sit down. And with that, my head went down and my hair was holding in all the blood. It just turned red on my hands. That's when my friends came running over, got me in their car, and drove me to Flushing Hospital."

By the time he got to the hospital, Denaro was semiconscious and in shock. He had actually been hit in the back of the head with a ricochet, the bullet ricocheting off the rearview mirror mounting arm on the inside of the windshield.

"I was in the hospital for two weeks. I was six hours in the emergency room. Basically what they were doing is taking bone fragments and pieces of glass out of the back of my head. The bullet had gone into my brain by one-eighth of an inch," deadly enough to have killed or most probably maimed.

Instead, he survived. As for his Air Force plans, they were put on permanent hold while he recovered.

November 27, 1976

It was a warm enough late November night that Joanne Lomino, eighteen, and her friend Donna DeMasi, seventeen, could hang out together on the porch of the Lomino home in the Bellerose section of Queens. It was a quiet residential area that saw little or no violence. The two girls had gone by bus and train into Manhattan to see a first run movie, then returned the same way and decided to stay outside for a while and enjoy the evening.

As the two girls sat on the porch, they could see a man in his early twenties dressed in Army fatigues casually walk up to the Lomino home. He began to ask the girls directions. Then, suddenly, he reached in the jacket pocket of his green, three-quarter-length coat. When it came out, the hand was holding a long-barreled revolver that began belching fire. Five times the gun barked, and twice bullets found their mark.

The first bullet tore into Donna's neck. The second round hit Lomino in the back. Then, as suddenly as he had appeared, the shooter was gone. The two girls were rushed to Long Island Jewish Hospital. Donna's wound proved treatable and she was soon listed in satisfactory condition. The same could not be said for Lomino. Placed in intensive care, she was diagnosed with a bullet wound to the spine that had severed her spinal cord and the motor function to her legs.

At the age of eighteen, she would be paralyzed for the rest of her life.

January 30, 1977

On the big screen at the Continental Theater in Forest Hills, Rocky Balboa collapsed into the arms of his opponent Apollo Creed at the end of their epic fifteen-round fight in *Rocky*.

Watching in the packed audience as the Oscar-winning screenwriter Sylvester Stallone's brilliant denouement played out, Christine Freund, a twenty-six-year-old Austrian immigrant who worked on Wall Street, and her fiancé and boyfriend of seven years, thirty-year-old John Diel, began to get into their coats and hats for their short walk. They looked up to see the movie end with Rocky in the arms of his beloved Adrienne.

Striding through the theater's ornate lobby with its high ceiling, Freund and Diel exited onto Austin Street, a brightly lit, jumping section of stores, restaurants, and upscale bars. They had seen the eight o'clock film, and the film let out around ten. The couple stopped at the Wine Gallery down the block for dinner. Afterward they walked a block and a half down to where Diel had parked his car in front of Station Square, directly opposite the Forest Hills Inn and the Forest Hills station of the Long Island Railroad.

The motor caught quickly but Diel let it warm up for a few moments in the January cold. Suddenly, three shots rang out from close range, shattering quiet and lives. To Diel, it seemed as if all at once the windows shattered around him. When he looked over, Freund was slumped in her seat. Losing no time, Diel shouted for help; no answer from the dark Queens street. He drove his car a few blocks up to 71st Avenue and Burns Street, where he blocked the intersection until frustrated motorists called police.

Two bullets had struck Freund, one in the shoulder, not fatal, and one in her head above the ear, which was. In a matter of moments her next big life event had turned from a wedding to a funeral. But while Freund's death bore an astonishing resemblance to the previous attacks, the police failed to link them; again, not unusual in serial killings.

"The shooting prompted the police to search records and memories for other apparently senseless killings in the past to see whether there was a possible link, they [the police] said," the *New York Times* reported.

The biggest problem in capturing a serial killer is the creative divide a homicide cop's mind has to skip in order to accept that what they are hunting this time is not your average run-of-the-mill killer but a killing machine that works with no seemingly apparent rhyme or reason. Cops have to be able to link the crimes successfully to even begin profiling or understanding what they hunt. If they don't, the killer keeps on going.

March 8, 1977

A junior at Columbia University majoring in Russian studies, Virginia Voskerichian was also a European immigrant, from Sofia, Bulgaria. For Virginia and her family—which included her parents, two sisters, and a brother—America had truly become the land of opportunity.

Slender, with dark eyes and high cheekbones, she

was walking down Dartmouth Street in Queens on her way home. The F train had let her off at the Continental Avenue stop, and it was only a few blocks' walk to get home. Whether Voskerichian knew that she was walking a half block away from where Freund had been slain is unclear. It is also unclear why police, knowing that some criminals actually do return to the scene of the crime, did not flood the area with uniformed police.

A stocky man jumped out at her from the shadows. The man took aim with a handgun, and Virginia's reflexive response was to bring the textbook up and cover her face. No problem for the Son of Sam. He cold-bloodedly walked up to her, put the gun against the cover of the book, and fired through it. The slug sliced through the pages, came out the back cover and ripped into Virginia's head, killing her instantly.

Five days later, on March 10, the NYPD gave a big press conference at their headquarters, One Police Plaza. Police Commissioner Mike Cod informed the assembled media that police had linked the same .44 caliber Bulldog revolver, made by the Charter Arms Company, to both the Lauria and Voskerichian homicides. The gun had also been used in two other shootings in Queens and the Bronx.

The police had a psycho on their hands, and they were very scared because they knew he was going to shoot again. They didn't know where or why, and they felt powerless to stop it. They did what they usually do when they don't know what to do. The police organized a task force. Called Operation Omega, its charge was to hunt down this murdering psycho.

April 17, 1977

At about midnight, Alexander Esau, twenty, called on his girlfriend, eighteen-year-old Valentina Suriani, to take her to a late movie. By 3:00 A.M. the movie was long over and the couple was parked alongside the service road of the Hutchinson River Parkway in the Bronx. Suriani was behind the wheel and Esau in the passenger seat when shots were fired through the closed driver's side windows. A resident of a nearby apartment building heard the shots and called police.

The cops arrived to find Suriani dead and Esau critically wounded with a bullet to the head. While he was whisked off to the hospital—he eventually survived—and Suriani was taken to the morgue, detectives discovered a note left by the killer at the crime scene. Addressed to Captain Joseph Borelli of Operation Omega, it said:

Dear Captain Joseph Borelli:

I am deeply hurt by your calling me a wemon hater. I am not. But I am a monster. I am the "Son of Sam" [author's emphasis]. I am a little brat.

When father Sam gets drunk he gets mean. He beats his family. Sometimes he ties me up to the back of the house. Other times he locks me in the garage. Sam loves to drink blood.

"Go out and kill," commands father Sam.

Behind our house some rest. Mostly young—raped and slaughtered—their blood drained—just bones now.

Papa Sam keeps me locked in the attic too. I can't get out but I look out the attic window and watch the world go by.

I feel like an outsider. I am on a different wavelength then everybody else—programmed too [sic] kill.

However, to stop me you must kill me. Attention all police: Shoot me first—shoot to kill or else keep out of my way or you will die!

Papa Sam is old now. He needs some blood to preserve his youth. He has had too many heart attacks. "Ugh, me hoot, it hurts, sonny boy."

I miss my pretty princess most of all. She's resting in our ladies house. But I'll see her soon.

I am the "Monster"—"Beelzebub"—the chubby *[author's emphasis] behemoth. I love to hunt. Prowling the streets looking for fair game—tasty meat. The wemon of Queens are prettiest of all. It must be the water they drink. I live for the hunt—my life. Blood for papa.*

Mr. Borelli, sir, I don't want to kill any-

more. No sur [sic], no more but I must, "honour thy father."

I want to make love to the world. I love people. I don't belong on earth. Return me to yahoos.

To the people of Queens, I love you. And I want to wish all of you a happy Easter. May God bless you in this life and in the next.

It is much easier with twenty-first century technology to analyze this letter, which would be unfair to expect of the NYPD of a quarter century ago. However, since many of them made their reputations on the case's solution, it is more than appropriate to point out that regardless of the year, the killer was telling the cops what he looked like when he used the word "chubby."

The references to Beelzebub and drinking blood refer to pagan devil worshiping customs that survive to the present day. It could mean the killer was a Satanist. That alone meant nothing. Satanists are not, as a rule, killers. They are, however, members of a group that when a criminal act is committed, the law looks at them as a gang.

Whoever the guy was, he had a flair for the dramatic. Naming himself the "Son of Sam" had a real flamboyance to it, a great name for a serial killer. And it was done consciously. Serial killers are boastful sorts; they feed off the headlines. Other patterns were also evident, yet not picked up by police at the time. Nearly all the assaults took place during the second half of the month. Police could have been on extra alert during those periods when the killer was bound to strike again.

Forensically, the letter and the envelope had been touched by so many people en route to the police captain that fingerprints were smudged and unusable. There was no way the killer's identity could be gleaned by the physical evidence. For a while police wisely did not leak the letter's contents to the press. It contained details that only the killer would know. If he was captured, it could be used to identify the proper suspect.

Secrecy, though, only goes so far in a big city police department. New York is no different. The contents of the letter began to leak out in the tabloids. Bold tabloid headlines blazed the name of the killer in black and white neon: the Son of Sam. It didn't help solve the case, but it did help sell newspapers.

"By June 1977, I was able to get a job," Denaro said. "I got a job at Citibank at their new building on East 53rd Street in Manhattan, manning their truck dock. But I knew I had to get out of New York."

Much like Kevin Bright, who knew he had to travel to heal after he was shot by BTK, Carl Denaro felt the same. He too packed his bags. But even before Denaro could begin his odyssey, trying to figure out what to do with the life that should not have been, Sam struck two more times.

July 30, 1977

Judy Placido had just graduated from a private Catholic high school in Queens. The plan was to take the Q train into Manhattan in the fall, where she would attend Pace University, a very good school.

That summer there were two big films to choose from: *Star Wars* and *Saturday Night Fever.* In New York City, disco was king. Discos throughout the five boroughs fed off *Fever*'s popularity. On Friday and Saturday nights, the really "in" Queens teens, like seventeen-year-old Judy Placido, went to the Alphas Disco on Northern Boulevard.

While at Alphas, Judy ran into a friend, Sal Lupo. Sometime after 3:00 A.M., Placido and Lupo left the disco together. They walked a half block to a car Lupo had borrowed from a friend. They got inside, Lupo behind the wheel and Placido in the passenger seat. For about ten minutes they talked, and then . . .

Four gunshots rang out, shattering the windows and two lives. When it was quiet again, Placido was critically injured with gunshot wounds to the neck, shoulder, and temple. She survived, as did Lupo, who was wounded in the right arm. Police ballistics tied the shooting to the previous ones that the Son of Sam had committed.

Once again the killer had done his work, and once again he got away. By then, the public had lost whatever confidence it may at one time have had for the much vaunted New York Police Department. Numerous films and television shows, not to mention novels and radio shows, had glamorized the department as a place where cops might be coarse, whatever their heritage, but were always smarter than anyone else in solving crimes.

The reality was, they were a bunch of outclassed boobs. Even at the distance of thirty years, the NYPD's collective IQ was clearly a lot less than Sam, who kept slipping through the (supposed) police dragnet set up for his capture. The reality was, this was also a post–Frank Serpico police department.

Frank Serpico was the greatest detective in the history of the NYPD. It was Serpico who exposed the police on the pad who bled good cops like him right out of the system. And then Serpico literally bled for the department when his backup team on an undercover drug deal did not come to his aid until he was shot by a drug dealer. A department stung to its quick by Serpico's proven allegations of corruption high up had to then deal with Sam's rampage.

July 31, 1977

It was the first time twenty-year-old Stacy Moskowitz, a secretary, had gone out with twenty-year-old Robert Violante, a clothing store salesman. Like many of the other victims, they had also gone to the movies, only this time the venue was the Bath Beach section of Brooklyn.

I lived there too.

Home for the summer from film school, I'd taken a job that my mother had arranged for me with a clothing manufacturer. I was an assistant buyer. The buyer was a guy a little older than me. He hated me because my future was in front of me and his was long behind. That summer was very hot, with a blackout—New York's second—sometime in the middle of it. That only added to the legitimate fear and paranoia that within the city's darkness Sam could be anywhere.

Bath Beach was a middle-class area, predominantly Italians who lived in private homes and a minority of Jews who lived in apartment building coops with faux elegant names like Harway Terrace and Contello Towers. They are still there. Some of us liked to neck on the service road of the Belt Parkway. It was dark, deserted in parts, very private. In the distance, less than a mile away, were the glittering lights of the Verrazano Narrows Bridge, "the longest suspension bridge in the world," Travolta's "Tony Manero" says to his date in *Saturday Night Fever*.

Violante and Moskowitz had parked on the Belt service road. At about 2:50 A.M., witnesses—other "neckers"—saw a man approach the Violante/Moskowitz car, go into a crouch—a two-handed combat style position—and fire four bullets through the open driver's side window. When the gun smoke cleared, Sam had long fled. Left behind in his vicious wake was Moskowitz, dead with two bullet wounds to the head.

Violante survived with a bullet to the head. Still conscious, he pumped his horn. There were actually people nearby who had seen the assault and were then coming to his aid. But he didn't see them. Violante opened the door and fell out of the car. He staggered to his feet and screamed, "Help me! Help me! Don't let me die."

By that time bystanders had finally gotten to him. Ambulances and police were summoned and both victims were taken to Kings County Hospital. Moskowitz was pronounced DOA, while Violante would survive the head wound that left him blind in one eye and partially blinded in the other for the rest of his life.

It was clear that whoever the Son of Sam was, he was exploiting the much maligned New York City transportation system. His ability to seemingly appear at will in the Bronx, Queens, and Brooklyn, and to immediately disappear after every shooting, meant that the Son of Sam was either the shrewdest person to ever use the New York City subways and buses, or he used a car to get from the crime scene du jour to his lair.

The break the police were looking for came from Cecilia Davis. She was nearby when Moskowitz and Violante were shot, and saw a man return to his parked car right after the shooting. The guy had gotten a ticket because he'd parked too close to a hydrant. The man tore the ticket off the windshield and threw it away, got in and drove off in a huff.

Unlike the NYPD, Cecilia Davis could add. Putting two and two together, she figured the guy was the Son of Sam. At first, of course, the police were skeptical. It couldn't be that simple, could it? Davis persisted with her claim. Finally, police decided to check it out. Sorting through the record of traffic tickets issued that night in Bath Beach near the Moskowitz/Violante crime scene, they came up with one that had been issued to a white Ford Galaxie that belonged to David Berkowitz, a postal worker who lived on Pine Street in Westchester County.

Soon, Operation Omega deployed a Special Weapons and Tactics Team (SWAT) that established a perimeter of armed officers around Berkowitz's neighborhood, which was north of the city. Then SWAT team members descended on Berkowitz just as he was getting into his car.

"Who are you?" one of the cops dumbly demanded, without advising him of his rights. Being the egotistical serial killer he was, Berkowitz flashed a crazy grin.

"I'm Sam," he admitted.

It was a much quoted line in police press releases and journalists' reports. Unfortunately, since Berkowitz said it before the cops read him his rights, it was inadmissible in court. The cops, though, got lucky, again. Had it not been for Davis coming forward, it is highly doubtful the tickets would have been run and Berkowitz identified. Second, like many serial killers, Berkowitz was a boastful, loquacious sort.

The "chubby behemoth"—Berkowitz is actually chubby, while certainly a criminal genius in his own mind—readily admitted to all the murders and assaults. But what was most amazing, his confession took all of thirty minutes! Standard interrogation interview techniques are to make the suspect reiterate his story over and over to get as many details as possible. It helps to fill in the blanks that lead to a successful prosecution. Why, then, didn't the NYPD use this standard technique, that is, make Berkowitz continue talking so as to be certain everything he said could be substantiated at trial?

Because he had confessed.

After a year-long investigation, and the formation of a special, elite 250-person task force, the cops arrested Berkowitz not because of some expert sleuthing, but over a stupid parking ticket. It was easier for them to just accept the confession and clear the cases. Whether Berkowitz had accomplices or might even be a part of some sort of satanic gang was not even considered.

Fortunes are made on the strangest of things, not the strangest being that the cop who gave Berkowitz the ticket got a promotion to detective for his actions. Many of the other upper echelon cops who worked the case also found themselves with professional kudos. And just who was the man they finally cornered and identified as the Son of Sam?

David Berkowitz had been adopted at birth by a Jewish couple. He grew up in a nice, middle-class Jewish home in the Bronx. In 1967, when he was fourteen, Berkowitz's mother died. Four years later his father remarried and moved to Florida. Eighteen-year-old David stayed behind in New York. Shortly afterward, he enlisted in the Army and served three years, with an honorable discharge.

Despite his honorable discharge, Berkowitz was breaking down emotionally. Back in the Bronx, he complained of persistent headaches; he thought people were out to kill him. Clearly, he had become schizophrenic. He began keeping a diary, in which he later claimed that he set 1,400 fires throughout the five boroughs in 1975, and knifed two women, who supposedly survived. However, Berkowitz's claims in his pre–Son of Sam diary cannot be taken seriously without the evidence to back them up.

While he would eventually exploit the New York City transportation system better than any killer in the city's history, he was not the Flash. He wasn't even Wally West. There was no way he could jet around NYC and commit, on average, three fires a day for 365 days, and sometimes do it in scattered parts of the outlying boroughs, as he claimed.

Berkowitz himself was consistent. Saving the state the cost of a trial, he copped a plea, admitting to everything the police had charged him with. Since the death penalty had been outlawed by the

Supreme Court as cruel and unusual punishment, Berkowitz got the law's maximum—twenty-five years to life with parole eligibility many years in the future. The first time he would even be considered for parole was in 2003, during the new Millennium.

It seemed a long way off. As for survivor Carl Denaro, he had trouble finding a place he could feel comfortable.

"From August 1978 to April 1980, I lived two years in Long Beach, California," he told me.

But the New Yorker in him yearned for home. When he came back, Denaro got into the work he does today. He became a phone auditor for large corporations, saving his clients millions in lost charges that make phone companies rich. He married, had a child, and divorced. But the shooting continued to dog him, and he thought about it, and paid attention to what Berkowitz had said over the years. He looked closely at the NYPD investigation and a parallel one done by a journalist who was particularly interested in the case.

"When I was shot, there were five shots taken. But only three bullets came from the same exact spot."

Denaro believes that the Son of Sam homicides involved more than one shooter. He also believes that the Lomino homicide and the DeMasi wounding prove out this point because the shooter was too far away to be accurate with both shots.

"The definition of the word is if there are more than two people involved, it's a conspiracy," he says.

Specifically, he believes that Berkowitz was telling the truth when he told Larry King in an interview that he was involved with Satanists and that the Son of Sam was actually a satanic conspiracy, of which Berkowitz was just one member. As proof, Denaro points out that not all the Sam homicides had the same M.O., which he believes indicates more than one person was involved.

"They were all done by a .44 caliber Bulldog, so there's your conspiracy, or is it?" Denaro says.

"You need to look at the forensics," I said.

Denaro says that "one of the ballistics detectives that worked on my bullet wrote in his report that the shooter was a 90-pound weakling or a female, based on the ballistics," which Denaro readily acknowledged he was not familiar with.

Denaro then sketched out a rough map of where he believed the shooters were the night he was shot. And I realized, "This guy really believes it was a conspiracy that shot him."

I hate conspiracies. Not only are they difficult to prove, most of the time they are a figment of someone's imagination, or a marketing ploy meant to eke out dollars from a tragic situation.

"Berkowitz was far from the leader," Denaro said. Asked if he was a Satanist, he replied, "Yes, but more in the vein of what we're reading about now in the news. Not in the Anton LaVey so much, but part of the 'I want to belong to a club and this is kind of neat,' know what I mean? But they do satanic rituals. Are they true Satanists? Me personally, I don't think they are. It's a good vehicle club to belong to, see what I'm saying?"

"Yes, I see what you are saying and it is very possible," I replied.

Denaro thought for a moment.

"I can reel off ten facts why there's more than one person involved."

"Why do you think they are alive?"

"Well, my famous line is, 'Being as I haven't discovered the cure for cancer, the only thing I can figure out is I am here to take care of my daughter.' "

"You've thought about it."

"Oh yeah! That's why when people say I shouldn't smoke, I say, 'Yeah, but I really shouldn't have gotten shot in the head either.' "

"Do you think there is an element of God in this?"

"Depends. I can give you two answers. The cynical one is if there's a God, it wouldn't have happened. The other answer was someone wanted me alive. I don't know why."

Outside, under a cold drizzle coming down from a slate gray sky, Denaro hopped into his Jaguar. We shook hands and he drove off.

As I walked to my car, I thought, So what? Legally, whether Berkowitz shot one or all, if he was part of a conspiracy, he's guilty of them all. As to whether there are those still alive who participated, so what? Convictions on decades old homicides without direct physical evidence or eyewitness testimony are almost impossible to obtain from any competent jury.

But I didn't say any of that. I didn't say any of that because even though I know the M.O. is not static in serial killings, even though I know most conspiracies are hokum, I believe Carl Denaro because he believes. Only a New Yorker could get shot by a serial killer, not be satisfied that the cops got the right one, and continue to investigate on his own.

In the end, what saved Carl Denaro's life, regardless of who shot him, was a ricocheting bullet on an errant path and a thorough knowledge of the streets of his borough. And it could have been me, I thought, it could have been me. All through the interview that thought was in the back of my mind.

It was many years ago and her looks could have

cost me my life. Cindy was a dark-haired brunette, hair cascading in waves to her shoulders. Her lush eighteen-year-old breasts were high, the curve of her waist hard from not yet having had a child. Her lips on mine were soft, her back spreading out beneath my hands as I felt for the bra strap under her red blouse.

I had parked my father's '73 Ford Fury (a gas eater) in a small, gravel-strewn lot behind Martin's Diner on Avenue M in Brooklyn with the sole intention of making out. Reaching under Cindy's shirt, my fingers sought out her bra clasp and . . . what was that? The shadow, outside the Fury's right rear window?

The streetlight was out; the only illumination came from the lights in the rear kitchen of the restaurant. Was someone moving out there? I looked back at Cindy and then it hit me—her hair. The cops said that the Son of Sam was partial to brunettes. Young brunettes. The girl I held in my arms was exactly Sam's type.

Just a few days before and a few miles away, Sam had ambushed a young couple. He killed the girl, Stacy Moskowitz, and blinded her twenty-year-old boyfriend Robert Violante. His weapon was a .44 caliber revolver. That much the police already knew. But who Son of Sam was, people had no idea. There was no telling when he would kill again. But he would. Everyone knew that, unless, of course, the cops finally caught him, and nobody had confidence in that.

Cindy lived someplace in the projects nearby. I dropped her and drove off, thankful we had not been the next victims of the Son of Sam.

*T*he next time anyone saw David Berkowitz was in 2003, when he came up for parole. By then, like many convicted killers, he had found God and was writing about it. His Web site explains it all. The serial killer has a Web site. *Network,* Paddy Chayefsky's nightmarish albeit hilarious cinematic vision of what the media would become sometime in the near future, has become reality.

Check it out: forgivenforlife.com. David's also been on Pat Robertson's *700 Club* proclaiming that God has forgiven him all of the misery he brought into the lives of innocent people. Whether that conversion is true or not, even Paddy hadn't thought of that.

During the end of an interview from Berkowitz's jail cell in 1997 with Larry King, this conversation took place. "Lieutenant Columbo" could not have done it any better.

KING: We're back [from break]. By the way, did you always act alone?

BERKOWITZ: Well, not really. Not totally like that.

KING: Were other people caught?

BERKOWITZ: No.

KING: They're still out there?

BERKOWITZ: Most have passed on. And—

KING: But they were involved in killing as well?

BERKOWITZ: They were . . .

KING: They got away with it?

BERKOWITZ: Well, no, they haven't gotten away with it and they won't. I—I . . .

KING: Do you think they're in hell?

BERKOWITZ: Some have lost their lives.

Berkowitz further explains his journey into the occult on his Web site:

> *In 1975 [prior to the Son of Sam murders], however, I met some guys at a party who were, I later found out, heavily involved in the occult. I had always been fascinated with witchcraft, Satanism, and occult things since I was a child. When I was growing up, I watched countless horror and satanic movies, one of which was* Rosemary's Baby. *That movie in particular totally captivated my mind.*

In the film, director Roman Polanski creates a mood of paranoid terror by having a satanic cult in NYC commandeer the body of innocent Mia Farrow to have Satan's child. What made the film so scary was, among other things, Polanski's casting of the archetypally bland Ralph Bellamy and an extremely subdued Ruth Gordon as two of the cult leaders. That, plus John Cassavetes's understated portrayal of Mia's husband, who goes over to the dark side, made it a really scary movie.

Even Polanski never thought of the only serial killer survivor ever, who drives a Jaguar, smokes filtered Marlboro Menthols, wears a stylish black leather jacket, and smells from existential cool.

*T*he letter from David Berkowitz arrived, care of my publisher. I had asked the convicted serial killer for an interview regarding this book. He replied that he had been busy helping another inmate on his case, but was very interested in my book. What other serial killers would I be covering? he asked.

He's still waiting for a reply.

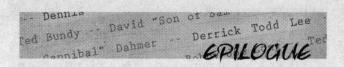

Adam Williams is the bartender at the Hickory BBQ. He makes the best Southern Comfort Manhattan imaginable.

"The key," says Adam, flipping the Boston shake thing better than Tom Cruise could ever hope to, "is not to let the Socol get too much of the ice in it. That thins it out. The reason you like a cocktail like this is because of the texture."

Adam chills a martini glass with ice. Then he pours out the ice and puts about two or three dashes of sweet vermouth at the very bottom. A little less than an ounce. Then, he puts four ounces of Socol in the Boston Shake with the ice. Next thing you know, I see him strain the Socol into the martini glass, hitting the sweet vermouth on the bottom and mixing naturally. He throws in a cherry and

it's the very best Southern Comfort Manhattan east
of the Mississippi River.

"So how was Louisville?" Adam asked me,
cleaning a glass and looking up at me.

I sipped, licked my lips, gave him the thumbs-up
and said, "I learned a lot."

"Like what?"

"I was afraid you'd ask me that . . . all right . . .
here goes . . . Don't order a mixed drink on a Friday night in a town in the deep South."

"Tell me something I don't know."

"All right. The people who survive serial killers do
so for a reason. They all have a few things in common. First and foremost, they make a decision *not*
to die. They are not going down without a fight, and
even when the fight is out of them, they are coming
back for more. It is their attitude that sustains them,
their belief that it just is not their time to die.

"Fortified by that, I believe the Divine enters the
frame. God does something that helps these people
survive. It is there in each and every case and it is
not too difficult to find it. That is, if you're open
enough to believe that to some extent we can control our own fate."

I took another sip. By that time Adam had turned
away from my ramblings and was serving someone
else. Could it be that simple? God helps those who
help themselves. Could that belief on the part of
the survivors, that it was *not* their time to die, have
triggered something, some spiritual mechanism or
intervention?

"Adam?"

"Yes, Fred," he said, looking up from wiping a glass.

"The hand that came down and that stopped the bike before it killed me was the same one that slowed Nita Neary down when she went into that room. It saved both our lives. It was God's hand. Had to be."

Adam thought for a moment. His right eyebrow went up.

"That would be nice wouldn't it?" he said, smiling.

APPENDIX 1

Hearing Concerning the Brain of Jeffrey Dahmer

After Jeffrey Dahmer was beaten to death in prison, his body was autopsied by a medical examiner who removed the brain from the body for further examination.

By the time the brain was ready to be returned to Dahmer's previously divorced parents, they were fighting over who would get it.

Upon his death, Dahmer had asked his father, Lionel, to have him cremated. Lionel wanted to honor that last request. But his mother wanted his brain preserved for science. Exactly what she thought science would find is hard to say. Dahmer's parents fought over their son's brain in court.

TRANSCRIPT OF PROCEEDINGS

(11:10 A.M., Mr. Dahmer via speaker phone.)

THE COUT [Columbia County Circuit Court Judge Daniel George]: All right. This is in the matter of the Estate of Jeffrey L. Dahmer. It's Case Number 94-PR-175. Appearing here today on a motion is Attorney Robert Fennig, is that correct?

MR. FENNIG: That's correct.

THE COURT: And you are appearing on behalf of Mr. Dahmer's mother Joyce Flint. And telephonically we have the father of Jeffrey Dahmer appearing personally. Your name is Lionel Dahmer, correct?

MR. DAHMER: Correct.

THE COURT: And are you there with an attorney, or are you on your own?

MR. DAHMER: I am on my own.

THE COURT: Okay. Any other appearances on behalf of any other party? Appears to be no other interested parties present in the courtroom.

We have a motion brought on by Mr. Fennig on behalf of Ms. Flint to have Jeffrey Dahmer's brain, as I understand it, turned over for purposes of scientific research. And based on correspondence that I have received from Lionel Dahmer, that is opposed by him. Is that correct, Mr. Dahmer?

MR. DAHMER: That is correct, Judge.

THE COURT: Okay. Mr. Fennig, before we went on the record here today I provided you with copies of the correspondence that the Court had received from

Lionel Dahmer. Although they had been received some days ago, I had not had an opportunity to see them until today, having been out of the office for the last week. Have you had an opportunity to review them?

MR. FENNIG: I have looked at them in the short time that I've been here. And I didn't get any of these sent to my office either, so this came as a—no surprise, but it—I didn't get any other notice that there would be opposition to the motion.

THE COURT: Okay.

MR. FENNIG: If I may?

THE COURT: Hang on just a moment. Mr. Dahmer, I want to touch base with you momentarily. Are you hearing Mr. Fennig?

MR. DAHMER: Barely. I can pick up a little bit of what he's saying. I think he said that he did not receive any correspondence. Of course, I've been at a business meeting, and I have sent you two faxes on September eighth and October first.

THE COURT: Okay. The—those have been received by the Court. But like I indicated, I didn't read them until today and they were provided to Mr. Fennig today. Mr. Fennig, are you prepared to go forward on your motion?

MR. FENNIG: Yes. Would it accommodate Mr. Dahmer if I got closer to the bar?

THE COURT: It may help to some degree. That's a fairly good microphone system, but it's obviously not perfect.

(Mr. Fennig approaches Bench)

MR. FENNIG: Mr. Dahmer, tell me if you can hear me better now.

MR. DAHMER: That's better.

THE COURT: Okay. Go ahead, then.

MR. DAHMER: Not perfect, but better.

MR. FENNIG: Well, we'll use what we have. This motion, as the papers indicate, is brought by Joyce Flint, the natural mother of the decedent in this matter.

After the autopsy, there remained brain and other tissue that was kept under the care and supervision of Dr. Robert W. Huntington at the University of Wisconsin Medical School. And he had these tissues under lock and key in one of the university hospitals in Madison.

Attempts were made to contact him by my client back in June with the thought of submitting this tissue for scientific study. It was indicated by Dr. Huntington that he would not release the tissue unless there was some authoritative decision made in that regard.

Mrs. Flint had been trying to contact Mr. Dahmer by telephone, and she used other parties to attempt to contact him. She never got a response by any of her phone calls. Now from what I have read from Mr. Dahmer, he denies getting any phone calls.

MR. DAHMER: That's not true.

MR. FENNIG: Would you let me finish, Mr. Dahmer?

MR. DAHMER: I didn't know that I wasn't supposed to respond in kind during the speaking.

THE COURT: Okay. Let me explain how we will run the procedure here today. First of all, Mr. Fennig is going to be allowed to present his argument. Then, Mr. Dahmer, I will hear from you before rendering any kind of decision. Because Mr. Fennig is the moving party, he will then have a final rebuttal opportunity after you have spoken.

MR. DAHMER: Okay, that's fine.

THE COURT: If you can keep your comments until I address you, and then I will hear your argument in total.

MR. FENNIG: I'll keep it quite brief. Based on nonresponses from Mr. Dahmer to Ms. Flint, it was suggested by contacting my office, and I represented her back in November immediately after the situation [Dahmer's murder] at the—at the jail. And I advised her that I would call Dr. Huntington and find out what it took to see to it that there may be a possibility of this occurring and under what circumstances Dr. Huntington would agree to it.

I was then made aware that Mrs. Flint had contacted the Georgetown University Medical Center, and this was made by reference from some folks out in California. Dr. Pincus has a widely known reputation in pathological neurological study. I was advised that Dr. Pincus had grant money to take care of the transportation and the research at hand. I wrote to Dr. Huntington about this. He said he would accept, if I could get a Court order with respect to that.

When I was here on the September sixth motion that was brought by all the claimants in the estate, I then secured a Court date for this motion and mailed it to all the interested parties as shown on my certificate of mailing. That was sent out, I believe, on the twelfth. And Mr. Dahmer got that, by acknowledgment in his letter, on the eighteenth.

I contacted Dr. Huntington and advised him that Dr. Pincus was available to accept this tissue. I contacted Dr. Huntington, who asked me for authority from Dr. Pincus. Dr. Pincus gave me a fax which I am showing to the Court now.

THE COURT: Let's have it marked as an exhibit.

MR. FENNIG: And it's, I believe, short enough to read.

(Exhibit marked)

THE COURT: Are there any other exhibits contemplated?

MR. FENNIG: Just one more.

THE COURT: Have it marked.

(Exhibit marked)

THE COURT: Okay. The first exhibit, for your benefit, Mr. Dahmer, is on letterhead from the Georgetown University Medical Center and bears the signature of Dr. Jonathan Pincus.

"I am grateful for this opportunity to study the brain of Jeffrey Daumer [sic]. It represents an unparalleled chance to possibly determine what neurological factors could have contributed to his bizarre criminal behavior.

"We will be glad to examine the brain tissue microscopically at Georgetown University. My grant will guarantee payment for the safe transportation of the brain in formaldehyde to my office at Georgetown University School of Medicine in Washington, D.C."

That's the extent of that exhibit. Go on, Mr. Fennig.

MR. FENNIG: Well, in answer, after I transmitted the fax of that letter to Dr. Huntington, he called me. We had a conversation, and I requested something in writing from his office with respect do Dr. Pincus's offer. And that is Exhibit 2. And that I believe is short enough to read, as well. If you would?

THE COURT: Exhibit Number 2 has been given to the Court. It is on University of Wisconsin Madison Medical School letterhead, bears the signature of Robert Huntington who is identified as an associate professor and who did the postmortem. It reads as follows:

"Dear Attorney Fennig, Thank you for forwarding the letter for Dr. Pincus. My original thought was to have the brain carefully studied at McLean Hospital in Boston. I am not acquainted with Dr. Pincus and his studies.

"The brain of Mr. Dahmer is to be studied carefully, as I would hope, I would also hope that scrupulous care be exercised against any premature conclusions.

"Mr. Dahmer's brain should, I would submit, be carefully compared against the range of brains from persons who exhibited normal and those showing severely antisocial behavior. In other words, I submit that concluding anything from this one brain by itself is perilous and antiscientific. If Dr. Pincus observes such scientific conditions, I would see no problem, on my part alone, in submitting that brain to his study. Sincerely."

And this bears Huntington's signature. Go on.

MR. FENNIG: Now the matter with respect to Mrs. Flint

is that we have gone through the cremation process, which happened within the past two or three weeks. And this ultimate disposition of what is left of the remains of her son would bring final closure to her, at least. And I believe there would be no other means to do it better than this.

It would satisfy her. It would not be in—against any interests of the public. In fact, I think the public may benefit from it. And I don't believe it would be in the—against any interests of Mr. Dahmer, the decedent himself, to have this done.

If you recall, by the means of his will—

And I bring that up because Mr. Lionel Dahmer made reference to it stating that any—any such disposal, either by cremation or the way we are asking for it, would be against what he set forth in his will. Mr.—He also indicated that he didn't want to have any funeral services. And Mr. Dahmer had, if you will recall, a memorial service within a couple of days after his death.

The point is, really, closure for Mrs. Flint. I think this would put her at rest. It would satisfy her to the point that some good has come out of all of this bad news in the last couple of years.

And for that reason her request is not outrageous. Her request is for the scientific—whatever scientific good can be made of this and I think deserves consideration by the Court.

THE COURT: Okay. Mr. Dahmer, I will hear from you.

MR. DAHMER: Okay. As to Joyce Flint contacting me personally, as she had said, she has had no response to her personal attempts. There were no personal attempts. I addressed that in my October first fax to you, Judge.

THE COURT: Okay. Mr. Dahmer, just for your information and to shorten up any kind of argument that we might have here, the fact that Joyce Flint may or may not have attempted to get your position on this matter or any kind of negotiations really has nothing to do with the Court's decision and isn't important to me.

MR. DAHMER: I feel it's irrelevant too. But I just wanted to answer that, remember when I broke in just a little bit ago.

THE COURT: Right. Okay, go ahead. On the merits of the matter, then.

MR. DAHMER: Okay. I think I probably summarized the main point of disregarding Jeff's instructions in his last testament, and I feel that that should take precedent. It's not a matter, I feel, of whether I do or don't want scientific study. I personally have strong feelings regarding the nonefficacious character of that proposal. But that's neither here nor there. I feel that the main point is what his last wishes were, and to violate that would be legally wrong.

THE COUT: Okay. Mr.—

MR. DAHMER: I could go on and on regarding the efficacious or nonefficacious character of the study, but I would rather not. I'm more of a writing person as opposed to an articulate on-the-spot verbal person, and I would rather put that in writing. But I want to emphasize at this moment the compliance with his last testament, as for anyone.

THE COURT: Mr. Fennig?

MR. FENNIG: If I can refer to his last testament. Page two of his will, paragraph four, he stated, "Upon my death I wish for the body to be cremated as soon as possible. I do not want a funeral ceremony to be performed before or after the cremation. No open casket. No headstone or marker."

If you will recall, Mr. Dahmer saw to a memorial service within days of the death of Jeffrey. And if he wants to go literally, he violated what he is now claiming would be a violation of the intentions of the decedent. So I think that's close to being doublespeak.

I think we do have a very good possibility that possibly something good can come of this by this scientific study. And for that reason, the motion has been made.

THE COURT: Mr. Dahmer, I'll give you one brief opportunity to respond if you wish.

MR. DAHMER: Okay. As to the funeral service, it was a private memorial service for my immediate family. And if he wants to argue to that point and seize upon that point, then he may want to prosecute me regarding that. But we are talking about the disposal of the wishes of Jeff for cremation of his body. The brain is part of his body. That's all.

THE COURT: Okay. The Court has heard argument concerning this matter. And I have received or actually will state now that I will receive Exhibit 1 and 2 from the two respective physicians or doctors involved in this matter, Dr. Huntington and Dr. Pincus.

The Court recognizes a rather unusual situation

here. It's one that I have certainly never encountered before and probably won't again. We do have competing interests from the two parents of the deceased. Those positions have been expressed here today. There is, in essence, a balancing test that the Court needs to perform.

I recognize the statement of the wishes of Jeffrey Dahmer. It was contained in a document entitled his Last Will and Testament. And although it is not technically a legal will from the standpoint of disposition of any of his property, it's not officially been admitted to probate. In fact, there was a stipulation and agreement by all parties that it wouldn't constitute a legal will of sorts with any sort of dispositive effect on what to do with his remains. Nonetheless, it is an expression that the Court gives some consideration to of the deceased's wishes as to what's to be done with his body.

And that certainly is a factor that the Court takes into consideration here.

I am also concerned with the issue of closure. This is a difficult situation in our human existence. It's a rather evil chapter. And I believe that it would be beneficial to the public and to all concerned that there be closure, and that this matter be resolved once and for all, and that we move on.

There also obviously is some interest from a scientific standpoint. And perhaps there is some good that could come from an otherwise particularly vile series of events. Perhaps there is some type of scientific research that could be conducted that might shed some kind of light on why acts of this nature occurred.

However, the Court is again looking at a balancing kind of test there in terms of the potential good and bad that could come from the research. There is or there are many different types of scientific research that can be conducted and many different levels of research that can occur from good to bad in range.

The Court is extremely concerned over the potential for exploitation of this type of research. I am very concerned and I have made some notes of my own, which pretty much coincided with the kinds of concerns raised by Dr. Huntington.

I am very fearful over the type of inquiry that's going to be made into this analysis. What sort of comparisons are going to be made? What sort of samples of population are we dealing with in terms of comparing the tissue from Mr. Dahmer's brain to other types of brains, brains from other individuals?

I don't know what is contemplated, and I am extremely concerned about the propriety of the handling of this issue and the avoidance of exploitation from the standpoint of any kind of pop research, pop psychology, that kind of thing. So what I would like to do, Mr. Fennig, is I would like something from Dr. Pincus that would enlighten this Court in greater detail as to where we are going with this.

Preferably I would like an opportunity to have him testify, which could be done by telephone just as Mr.

Dahmer is participating here today. What I would like you to do is contact Dr. Pincus and find out what his availability is and find out whether he would be willing to submit a more detailed analytical approach as to what direction he intends to take with his analysis, and preferably whether he would be willing to testify by telephone.

And after hearing that I would be inclined to make a decision with respect to what to do with this material. Because at this point to just carte blanche say, here you go, do with it as you wish, is beyond what this Court is willing to tolerate. And we could end up with a situation that digresses considerably from the purpose that is contemplated.

So, Mr. Dahmer . . .

MR. DAHMER: Yes?

THE COURT: . . . I will be getting some kind of feedback from Attorney Fennig concerning Dr. Pincus's position, at which time we will be doing some scheduling of another hearing of this nature. And between now and then I would also invite you to, as you indicated during your argument here today, present further written argument to me, feeling that you can do so in a more effective manner than speaking.

MR. DAHMER: Well, the fact is I've been sitting up at night in a motel room typing.

THE COURT: I recognize the difficulty in terms of responding—

MR. DAHMER: Thank you.

THE COURT:—extemporaneously here today. So between now and the next hearing, if in fact we are to have another hearing, I would contemplate such depending on what Dr. Pincus is going to tell us. Between now and then you may submit anything in writing.

You have received notice from Mr. Fennig of today's proceedings, correct?

MR. DAHMER: Yes.

THE COURT: So you have his address. Anything you send to the Court should likewise be copied to Mr. Fennig.

MR. DAHMER: I certainly will.

THE COURT: That will terminate, then, today's proceedings. Mr. Fennig, if you would contact my scheduling clerk after you've received information from Dr. Pincus and arrange for another hearing of this nature, she will be able to accommodate you. Any questions?

MR. FENNIG: Just one thing. I think what I will also get will be a vitae with respect to Dr. Pincus's qualifications.

MR. DAHMER: I'm sorry. I can't hear that.

THE COURT: What he's saying is he would attempt to get a vitae—curriculum vitae, a resume, whatever you want to call it—from Dr. Pincus.

That would be very helpful for the Court, as well.

MR. FENNIG: And I will send it to Mr. Dahmer prior to the hearing.

THE COURT: Anything Mr. Fennig sends to the Court will likewise be sent to you, Mr. Dahmer. I assume he has your proper address.

MR. DAHMER: Yes, it is. Thank you.

THE COURT: That will conclude today's proceedings.

MR. DAHMER: Thank you, Judge.

MR. FENNIG: Thank you.

Dr. Pincus eventually testified by phone in Judge George's court over the matter of Dahmer's brain. The judge, who had studied physiological psychology as an undergraduate, wasn't convinced of the fundamental worth of releasing Dahmer's brain to the science men.

"Then in considering how the guy died—you're talking about doing research on a salvaged brain from someone whose skull was crushed by a steel bar by a very large, powerful man that beat him to the point where people who were transporting him couldn't even recognize who it was," George told a reporter for the *Portage Daily Register*.

Judge Daniel George then ordered the brain of Jeffrey Dahmer destroyed.

APPENDIX 11

BTK Correspondence Taunts Cops and Media

Dennis Rader liked to taunt police and reporters. Periodically during his thirty year criminal career, Rader, in his BTK guise, sent letters, notes, and poetry to cops and reporters. It gave him a feeling of tremendous power and control.

BTK's first letter arrived at police headquarters in October 1974. The cops knew immediately it was genuine because the writer gave details of the Otero family murders that only the killer could know.

> I write this letter to you for the sake of the tax payer as well as your time. Those three dudes you have in custody are just talking to get publicity for the Otero murders. They know nothing at all. I did it by myself and with no ones help. There has been no talk either. Let's put this straight . . . I'm sorry this

happen to society. They are the ones who suffer the most.

It is hard to control myself. You probably call me "psychotic with sexual perversion hang-up." When this monster enters my brain I will never know. But, it here to stay. How does one cure himself? If you ask for help, that you have killed four people, they will laugh or hit the panic button and call the cops.

I can't stop it so the monster goes on, and hurt me as well as society. Society can be thankful that there are ways for people like me to relieve myself at time by day dreams of some victims being torture and being mine. It a big complicated game my friend of the monster play putting victims number down, follow them, checking up on them waiting in the dark, waiting, waiting . . . the pressure is great and sometimes he run the game to his liking.

Maybe you can stop him. I can't. He has aready chosen his next victim or victims. I don't who they are yet. The next day after I read the paper, I will know, but it to late. Good luck hunting.

YOURS, TRULY
GUILTILY

The killer failed to sign. Then, as a seeming afterthought:

P.S. Since sex criminals do not change their M.O. or by nature cannot do so, I will not change mine. The code words for me will be . . . Bind them, torture them, kill them, B.T.K., you see he at it again. They will be on the next victim.

Not only did Dennis Rader have the absolute hubris to give himself a nifty, tabloid-ready name, he even punctuated it correctly! That was a tip-off if anyone with a brain had been paying attention. Whoever had written the letter had deliberately disguised their educational level.

On January 31, 1978, the *Wichita Eagle* received a poem from BTK based on the nursery rhyme "Curley Locks." In the original:

Curley Locks, Curley Locks, Wilt thou be mine?

Thou shalt not wash dishes, nor yet feed the swine
But sit on a cushion and sew a fine seam
And feed upon strawberries, Sugar and cream.

Here's the BTK version. Much briefer, it refers to the killing of Shirley Vian:

Shirley Locks

Shirley Locks, Shirley Locks, will you be mine

BTK claimed that his next poem would be about victim Nancy Fox, who he murdered on December 8, 1977. Then, on February 9, 1978, BTK sent a four page letter to KAKE-TV. In it, he claimed responsibility for seven murders and threatened to kill again. Included was this poem:

Oh! Death to Nancy

What is this taht [sic] I can see
Cold icy hands taking hold of me for Death has
   come, you all can see.
Hell has open its gate to trick me.
Oh! Death, Oh! Death, can't you spare me, over
   for another year!
I'll stuff your jaws till you can't talk
I'll blind [sic] your leg's [sic] till you can't walk
I'll tie your hands till you can't make a stand.
And finally I'll close your eyes so you can't see
I'll bring sexual death unto you for me.

Police later worked confidentially with a Wichita State University literature professor who analyzed a 1920s folk song entitled "Oh Death." BTK's, "Oh! Death to Nancy," was based on the original folk song, which clearly carried significance to the killer.

In April 1979, Dennis Rader waited inside the home of sixty-three-year-old Anna Williams. Losing patience, he left before she got home. Several weeks later, BTK sent her this poem:

Oh Anna, Why Didn't You Appear
It was perfect plan of deviant pleasure so bold
*   on that Spring nite*
My inner felling hot with propension of the new
*   awakening season*
Warn, wet with inner fear and rapture, my plea-
*   sure of e e*
entanglement, like new vines at night.

Along with the poem were some items BTK had stolen from Williams's home. KAKE-TV reportedly received a similar package. This was the last of the officially recognized BTK letters until March 19, 2004, when BTK resurfaced again with a letter to the *Wichita Eagle*. It contained a copy of Vicki Wegerle's driver's license and three photos BTK had taken of her body right after he killed her.

On May 5, 2004, KAKE-TV received another letter from BTK and turned it over to police. This letter contained a list of chapter titles from *Crime Library*'s feature story on the BTK case, which had been the only BTK feature story on the Internet at that time. However, BTK modified the original *Crime Library* chapter titles to suit his own purposes:

THE BTK STORY

1. *A SERIAL KILLER IS BORN*
2. *DAWN*
3. *FETISH*

On June 17, 2004, another letter was found in a mechanical engineering book in the drop box of the Wichita Public Library. Authorities did not reveal the letter's entire contents but did confirm that, among other things, the letter detailed some of the events surrounding the 1974 Otero murders.

On October 22, 2004, the thirtieth anniversary of BTK's first communication with authorities, a suspicious letter was left at a UPS drop box outside the OmniCenter building in Wichita, Kansas. Authorities confirmed it was a BTK communication. The letter's contents and the identity of the person who alerted police to its location remain unclear.

On November 30, 2004, Wichita police issued a press release offering a great deal of background information about BTK, which he himself had supplied in his communications. Then, in mid-December 2004, a suspicious-looking white plastic bag wrapped in rubber bands was found in Murdock Park. When it was opened, police found a driver's license belonging to Nancy Fox along with other objects belonging to victims.

On January 25, 2005, a tip-off to KAKE-TV led to the detection of "a suspicious package" on "a dirt road that runs between 69th and 77th Street North," the television station revealed in an article on its Web site. Sent by BTK, the package contained a Post Toasties cereal box and several items of jewelry.

Earlier in January and again in February, a postcard was sent by BTK to the television station. Jeanene Kiesling reported in her KAKE-TV Web site article that the two BTK postcards were similar in layout and directed the reader to the Post Toasties cereal box that was found on January 25. BTK then sent KAKE-TV *another* postcard, thanking them for their quick response.

Several weeks later in February, Fox News KSAS-TV affiliate received a padded manila envelope sent by BTK. It contained a necklace, a letter, and another unidentified item. The package, which was BTK's seventh communication, was handed over to the police for analysis. Police later concluded that the necklace belonged to one of BTK's victims.

That same week, Kiesling reported for the first time the entire list of chapters BTK sent to KAKE-TV in May 2004. Loosely based on *Crime Library*'s BTK story, the BTK-authored chapter list was not made public earlier because the police did not want it to hamper the ongoing investigation.

But BTK's time had run out. The state drafted a

document that they personally presented to Dennis Rader:

Complaint against Dennis Rader

IN THE DISTRICT COURT OF KANSAS
EIGHTEENTH JUDICIAL DISTRICT
SEDGWICK COUNTY, CRIMINAL DEPARTMENT

THE STATE OF KANSAS)
Plaintiff,)
vs.)
) Case No.
DENNIS L. RADER,)
W/M, DOB: 03/09/45,)
)
Defendant.)

_____)

COMPLAINT/INFORMATION

COUNT ONE
COMES NOW KIM T. PARKER, a duly appointed, qualified and acting Deputy District Attorney of the 18th Judicial District of the State of Kansas, and for and on behalf of said State gives the court to understand and be informed that in the County of Sedgwick, and State of Kansas, and on or about the 15th day of January, 1974, A.D., one DENNIS L. RADER did then and there unlawfully, kill a human being, to-wit: Joseph Otero, maliciously, willfully, deliberately and with premeditation by strangulation and or asphyxiation, inflicting injuries from which the said Joseph Otero did die on or about January 15, 1974;

Contrary to Kansas Statutes Annotated 21-3401, Murder in the First Degree, Class A Felony [L. 1969, ch. 180, 21-3401; L. 1972, ch. 112, 1; July 1], Count One

COUNT TWO

and on or about the 15th day of January, 1974, A.D., in the County of Sedgwick, State of Kansas, one DENNIS L. RADER did then and there unlawfully, kill a human being, to-wit: Julie Otero, maliciously, willfully, deliberately and with premeditation by strangulation, inflicting injuries from which the said Julie Otero did die on or about January 15, 1974;

COUNT THREE

and on or about the 15th day of January, 1974, A.D., in the County of Sedgwick, State of Kansas, one DENNIS L. RADER did then and there unlawfully, kill a human being, to-wit: Josephine Otero, maliciously, willfully, deliberately and with premeditation by strangulation, inflicting injuries from which the said Josephine Otero did die on or about January 15, 1974;

COUNT FOUR

and on or about the 15th day of January, 1974, A.D., in the County of Sedgwick, State of Kansas, one DENNIS L. RADER did then and there unlawfully, kill a human being, to-wit: Joseph Otero, Jr., maliciously, willfully, deliberately and with premeditation by strangulation and or asphyxiation, inflicting injuries from which the said Joseph Otero, Jr. did die on or about January 15, 1974;

Contrary to Kansas Statutes Annotated 21-3401, Murder in the First Degree, Class A Felony [L. 1969, ch. 180, 21-3401; L. 1972, ch. 112, 1; July 1], Count Two

Contrary to Kansas Statutes Annotated 21-3401, Murder in the First Degree, Class A Felony [L. 1969, ch. 180, 21-3401; L. 1972, ch. 112, 1; July 1], Count Three

Contrary to Kansas Statutes Annotated 21-3401, Murder in the First Degree, Class A Felony [L. 1969, ch 180, 21-3401; L. 1972, ch. 112, 1; July 1], Count Four

COUNT FIVE

and on or about the 4th day of April, 1974, A.D., in the County of Sedgwick State of Kansas, one DENNIS L. RADER did then and there unlawfully, kill a human being, to-wit: Kathryn Bright, maliciously, willfully, deliberately and with premeditation by strangulation and stabbing, inflicting injuries from which the said Kathryn Bright did die on April 4, 1974;

COUNT SIX

and on or about the 17th day of March, 1977, A.D., in the County of Sedgwick, State of Kansas, one DENNIS L. RADER did then and there unlawfully, kill a human being, to-wit: Shirley Vian, maliciously, willfully, deliberately and with premeditation by strangulation, inflicting injuries from which the said Shirley Vian did die on March 17, 1977;

COUNT SEVEN

and on or about the 8th day of December, 1977, A.D., in the County of Sedgwick, State of Kansas, one DENNIS L. RADER did then and there unlawfully, kill a human being, to-wit: Nancy Fox, maliciously, willfully, deliberately and with premeditation by strangulation, inflicting injuries from which the said Nancy Fox did die on December 8, 1977;

Contrary to Kansas Statutes Annotated 21-3401, Murder in the First Degree, Class A Felony [L. 1969, ch. 180, 21-3401; L. 1972, ch. 112, 1; July 1], Count Five

Contrary to Kansas Statutes Annotated 21-3401, Murder in the First Degree, Class A Felony [L. 1969, ch. 180, 21-3401; L. 1972, ch. 112, 1; July 1], Count Six

Contrary to Kansas Statutes Annotated 21-3401, Murder in the First Degree, Class A Felony [L. 1969, ch. 180, 21-3401; L. 1972, ch. 112, 1; July 1], Count Seven

COUNT EIGHT

and on or about the 27th day of April, 1985, A.D., to the 28th day of April, 1985, A.D., in the County of Sedgwick, State of Kansas, one DENNIS L. RADER did then and there unlawfully, kill a human being, to-wit: Marine Hedge, maliciously, willfully, deliberately and with premeditation by strangulation, inflicting injuries from which the said Marine Hedge did die on April 27, 1985;

COUNT NINE

and on or about the 16th day of September, 1986, A.D., in the County of Sedgwick, State of Kansas, one DENNIS L. RADER did then and there unlawfully, kill a human being, to-wit: Vicki Wegerle, maliciously, willfully, deliberately and with premeditation by strangulation, inflicting injuries from which the said Vicki Wegerle did die on September 16, 1986;

COUNT TEN

and on or about the 18th day of January, 1991, A.D., to the 19th day of January, 1991, A.D., in the County of Sedgwick, State of Kansas, one DENNIS L. RADER did then and there unlawfully, kill a human being, to-wit: Dolores E. Davis, maliciously, willfully, deliberately and with premeditation by strangulation, inflicting injuries from which the said Dolores E. Davis did die on January 19, 1991;

Contrary to Kansas Statutes Annotated 21-3401, Murder in the First Degree, Class A Felony [L. 1969, ch. 180, 21-3401; L. 1972, ch. 112, 1; July 1], Count Eight

Contrary to Kansas Statutes Annotated 21-3401, Murder in the First Degree, Class A Felony [L. 1969, ch. 180, 21-3401; L. 1972, ch. 112, 1; July 1], Count Nine

Contrary to Kansas Statutes Annotated 21-3401(a), Murder in the First Degree, Off-Grid Person Felony, [L. 1969, ch. 180, 21-3401; L. 1972, ch. 112, 1; July 1, L. 1989, ch. 87, 1, L. 1990, ch. 100, 2] Count Ten

all of the said acts then and there committed being contrary to the statutes in such cases made and provided and against the peace and dignity of the State of Kansas.

BIBLIOGRAPHY

The New York Times, July 14-16, 18-19, 1966, News section

Ibid. April 6-7, 1967, News section

Ibid. April 16, 1967, News section

Ibid. June 6, 1967, News section

Ibid. Jan. 5, 1969, International section

Ibid. Jul. 30, 1976, News section

Ibid. Nov. 28, 1976, News section

Ibid. Mar. 9, 1977, News section

Ibid. April 18, 1977, News section

Ibid. Aug. 1, 1977, News section

Ibid. Aug. 12, 1977, News section

Ibid. Jan. 31, 1977, News section

Wichita Eagle, Oct. 16, 2005, News section

Boivin, Janet RN. Nov. 15, 1999. "Remembering Richard Speck's Victims." *Nursing Spectrum.* Available from World Wide Web: http://community.nursingspectrum.com/Magazine Articles/article.cfm?AID=17

CNN.com. Jun. 27, 2005, Law Center section. Available from World Wide Web: http://www.cnn.com/2005/LAW/06/27rader. transcript/index.html

Ferguson, Paul. 2006. "Squabble Over Dahmer's Brain." *Portage Daily Register.* Available from World Wide Web: http://portage.scwn.com/articles/2004/11/27/ news/news2.txt

Lohr, David. 2006. "Ted Bundy: The Poster Boy of Serial Killers." *Crime Magazine* Web site. Available from World Wide Web:\ http://crimemagazine.com/ted_bundy.htm

Oliveras Cunanen, Belinda. Jan. 5, 2004. *Political Tidbits: Filipino Nurses Preferred.* Philippines. INQ7.Net. Available from World Wide Web:
http://www.inq7net/opi/2004/jan/05/opi_bocunanan-1.htm

Prud*Home, Alex. Aug 5, 1991. "The Little Flat of Horrors." New York: New York. *Time* magazine. Available from World Wide Web:
http://time-roxy.yaga.com/time/archive/preview/0,10987,973550,00.html?internalid=ACA

Psychology, Department of. 2005. *Jeffrey Dahmer.* Radford: VA. Radford University. Available from World Wide Web:
http://www.radford.edu/~maamodt/Psyc%20405/serial%20killers/Dahmer,%20Jeff.htm

Psychology, Department of. 2000. *Sexual Disorders: the Case of Jeffrey Dahmer.* Henderson: SC. Dahmer Vance-Granville Community College. Available from World Wide Web:
http://oit.vgcc.edu/psy281/Projects.htm

Summers, Chris. 2006. "Jeffrey Dahmer, The Milwaukee Cannibal." *BBC* Web site. Available from World Wide Web:
http://www.bbc.co.uk/crime/caseclosed/dahmer1.shtml

Unknown. *Psychiatric Testimony of Jeffrey Dah-
    mer.* 2001. *Criminal Profiling* Web site. Available
    from World Wide Web:
    http://www.criminalprofiling.com/Psychiatric-
    Testimony-of-Jeffrey-Dahmer_s115.html